GEORGE III
At Home

GEORGE III
At Home

Nesta Pain

EYRE METHUEN
LONDON

First published 1975
Copyright © Nesta Pain 1975
Printed in Great Britain for
Eyre Methuen Ltd
11 New Fetter Lane, London EC4P 4EE
by The Bowering Press Ltd
Plymouth

ISBN 0 413 26590 0

Contents

Contents

[9]

Illustrations

Genealogical Table showing the House of Hanover

page 10

Engraving of Buckingham House by William Westaw

endpapers

Acknowledgements and thanks for permission to reproduce photographs are due to the Mansell Collection for the endpapers; to Christie's for the frontispiece; to the National Portrait Gallery for plates 1b, 6, 10, 11 and 12; to the British Museum for plates 1a and 7a; to the Victoria and Albert Museum for plate 9. Plates 2, 3, 4, 5, 7b and 8 are reproduced by gracious permission of Her Majesty the Queen.

The genealogical table was drawn by Edgar Holloway.

Foreword

George III lived to be over eighty years old and he was on the throne for nearly sixty years, so that many public events of importance took place during his reign. As king, he was concerned in them, and in a formal biography they must all be dealt with in fair detail. In consequence, private life tends to be squeezed into very small compass. It is this gap, inevitable in a modern one-volume biography, which I have attempted to fill.

London
July 1974   NESTA PAIN

THE HOUSE OF HANOVER

GEORGE I
King of Great Britain
1660-1727
m.1682 Sophie-Dorothea
of Brunswick-Luneburg
1666-1726

Sophia-Dorothea 1685-1757
m.1706 Frederick William I
King of Prussia

GEORGE II
King of Great Britain
1683-1760
m.1705 Caroline of Anspach 1683-1737

Frederick Prince of Wales
1707-1751
m.1736 Augusta of Saxony
1719-1772

William Duke of
Cumberland
1721-1765

Maria
1722-1772
m.1740 Frederick II
Landgrave of Hesse-Cassel
d.1785

Louise
1724-1751
m.1743 Frederick V
King of Denmark

Anne
1709-1759
m. William IV
Prince of Orange

Amelia
1711-1786

Caroline
1713-1757

George
1717-1718

Augusta
1737-1813
m.1764 Charles
Duke of Brunswick-
Wolfenbüttel
1735-1806

GEORGE III
King of Great Britain
1738-1820
m.1761 Charlotte of
Mecklenburg-Strelitz
1744-1818

William
Duke of Gloucester
1743-1805
m.1766 Maria Waldegrave
1736-1807

Henry
Duke of Cumberland
1745-1790
m.1771 Anne Horton
1742-1808
Without issue

Caroline-Matilda
1751-1775
m.1766 Christian VII
King of Denmark

Edward
Duke of York
1739-1767

Elizabeth
1741-1759

Louisa
1749-1768

Frederick
1750-1765

Frederick Duke of York
1763-1827
m.1791 Frederika
of Prussia 1767-1820
without issue

GEORGE IV
Prince Regent
later King of
Great Britain
1762-1830
m.1795 Caroline of
Brunswick-Wolfenbüttel
1768-1821
d. of Charles (above).

WILLIAM IV
Duke of Clarence
King of Great Britain
1765-1837
m.1818 Adelaide
of Saxe-Meiningen
1792-1849
Without issue

Charlotte
1766-1828
m.1797 Frederick
King of
Würtemberg

Edward
Duke of Kent
1767-1820
m.1818 Victoria of
Saxe-Coburg

Augusta
1768-1840

Elizabeth
1770-1840
m.1818
Frederick of Hesse-
Homburg
Landgrave of Hesse-
Homburg
1769-1829
Without issue

Ernest Duke of
Cumberland
King of Hanover
1771-1851
m. Frederika of
Mecklenburg-Strelitz
1778-1841
Royal Line of Hanover

Augustus
Duke of Sussex
1773-1843
m.(1)1793 Lady
Augusta Murray
1768-1830
(2)1831 Lady
Cecilia Buggin
1785-1873

Adolphus Duke
of Cambridge
1774-1850
m.1818 Augusta
of Hesse-
Homburg
1797-1889

Mary
1776-1857
m.1816 William
Duke of Gloucester
1776-1834
Son of
William and Maria
Waldegrave

Sophia
1777-1848

Octavius
1779-1783

Alfred
1780-1782

Amelia
1783-1810

VICTORIA
Queen of Great Britain
Empress of India
1819-1901
m.1840
Albert of Saxe-Coburg-Gotha
1819-1861

Charlotte
1796-1817
m.1816 Leopold
Prince of Saxe-Coburg
Leopold I of Belgium

I

Unhappy Families

George III was happier in his relationship with his father than
most of his family, for in general the Hanoverians were hostile
to their eldest sons. George I disliked his son, the future
George II, so much that he seriously considered having him
kidnapped and taken overseas, and George II, who once remarked
that he hated to have children pattering about the house, left
his son Frederick behind in Hanover when he was only seven
years old. It was not until he was twenty-one that the pressure
of public opinion forced the King to allow him to come to
England.

Better acquaintance only served to increase their mutual dislike. 'Puppy', the King would call his son, or 'monster', and once
'the greatest villain that ever was born'. His wife, Queen Caroline,
joined him in equally vigorous abuse. 'The mean fool! The poor-
spirited beast,' she exclaimed one day at breakfast. 'My dear
first-born is the greatest ass, and the greatest beast in the whole
world.' She would often curse the hour of his birth and wish
him in the 'lowest hole in hell'. 'Pray, Mamma,' said the gentle
Princess Caroline, 'do not throw away your wishes on what cannot happen, but wish he may die and that we may all go about
with smiling faces and glad hearts – and of course crêpe and
hoods.'

Frederick's upbringing may account for at least some of his
later faults of character, for he was left in the charge of tutors who
seem to have taught him nothing but to drink and gamble and
lead a generally dissolute life. It might not have mattered so

much if he had been likeable, but he was not. He was never popular and he was generally thought to be a hypocrite and a liar.

When he was in his late twenties, he asked his father's permission to marry, partly, no doubt, because on marriage his allowance would be increased – a fact which probably also accounts for his father's reluctance to agree. However, he could not refuse indefinitely and the available Protestant princesses were considered in turn. The choice was small. The Prince objected to the Princess of Denmark on the grounds that she was 'crooked and a dwarf', and the King did not fancy the princesses of Prussia, saying that they had a 'madman' for their father and he did not think 'engrafting' his 'half-witted coxcomb upon a madwoman would mend the breed'. In the end the King decided that Augusta of Saxe-Gotha would do best, and Frederick gracefully agreed, saying that whoever his Majesty thought a proper match would be agreeable to him.

Princess Augusta was only seventeen years old and spoke no English and little French. She was far from being a beauty, but she looked healthy and good-natured, and her only serious defect was her figure, which was described as 'a good deal awry'. She gave such an impression, however, of mildness and modesty that even her parents-in-law found themselves unable to object to her, and anything she did wrong was always blamed on Frederick. 'Poor creature!' the Queen would say, 'if she were to spit in my face, I should only pity her for being under such a fool's guidance and wipe it off.' But the princess's manners may have been deceptive, for she became a formidable woman in later life.

The future George III was the second child of the marriage, the first being a daughter. He was born prematurely on 4 June 1738 and was rather delicate in his early years. He was, however, luckier in his parents than his father had been, for neither of them was hostile to him and Frederick even took an interest in his development. Frederick loved music himself and encouraged his children to appreciate it, and he also had a passion for amateur theatricals. He engaged professional directors for the plays his children acted, and one French guest at his house was very taken aback to find himself faced with a choice of playing rounders or sitting through a performance of Addison's *Cato* performed by the children. He was lucky not to be asked to help the children weed their gardens.

Frederick took trouble over his son's formal education as well, and reasonably competent tutors were engaged – one of them at least, George Scott, was a definite success. The boys were taught Latin, French and German, history, mathematics and religion, and polite accomplishments such as music and dancing. The progress achieved was eccentric, for at eleven George was still having difficulty in reading and writing English, but could make a fair shot at writing Latin verse. Military history was his best subject and this – particularly the minutiae of military uniforms – became an interest which lasted his life. Athletics were also encouraged by Frederick and the boys played rounders, ninepins, and above all, cricket, sometimes joined by their father.

Frederick's marriage had been neither happy nor unhappy. He was consistently unfaithful to his wife, but both took this as a matter of course, and they remained on reasonably good terms. Lord Bute, who was to play so large a part in George's later life, came on the scene as a result of a meeting with Frederick at Egham races. Rain began to fall, both men went into a tent for shelter and Frederick decided to pass the time by playing whist. Lord Bute was asked to make up a four and Frederick took a fancy to him – so much so that he invited Lord Bute to visit him at his country house. Here he met the Princess of Wales, who took an even stronger fancy to him.

Lord Bute was a remarkably handsome man, but vain, pompous and self-important, and when Frederick appointed him a Lord of the Bedchamber, he soon became more haughty than ever. 'His bows grew more theatric,' said Horace Walpole, 'and the beauty of his leg was constantly displayed in the eye of the poor captivated Princess.' She could not have admired it more than he did himself for he is said to have passed many hours a day 'contemplating' its symmetry. It was thought the best leg in London.

Frederick had no objection to Lord Bute's attentions to his wife and sometimes, before turning down a secluded avenue at Kew with his latest mistress, he would tell them to take a walk together as well. When the Prince died a year later, 'they walked more and more', said Walpole, 'in honour of his memory'.

Frederick's opinion of Lord Bute's abilities had never been particularly high, for although Bute had always made a great show of learning, his knowledge, apart from botany, was second-hand and second-rate. He made the most of what he had, however, by talking in slow and measured tones, as if imparting some weighty matter; he had an air of 'lofty ignorance', said Horace Walpole. Frederick remarked to him one day, with a flash of real penetration, 'Bute, you would make an excellent ambassador in some proud little court where there is nothing to do.' He would have been in his element.

Frederick had always been fond of gardening – this was a bond with Bute – and it was while he was helping to construct a new walk designed by himself for his country house at Kew, that he caught the chill which ended his life.

As he lay dying, Dunoyer, the dancing-master, who was an old friend, stayed at his bedside and played the fiddle to him. Suddenly Frederick clutched his stomach, whispered, 'Je sens la mort', and died. It was March 1751 and George was not yet thirteen.

Frederick was not fortunate in his obituaries, which ranged from the well-known: 'Here lies poor Fred, Who was alive and is dead, There's no more to be said', through his brother, the Duke of Cumberland's dry remark that it was a great blow to the country, but he hoped it would recover in time, to a distinctly strange address delivered at the Mayfair Chapel.

'His Royal Highness,' said the preacher, 'had no great parts, but he had great virtues; indeed they degenerated into vices; he was very generous, but I know his generosity has ruined a great many people; and then his condescension was such that he kept very bad company.'

To his son, George, if to nobody else, Frederick was a serious loss. For one thing, his widow, the Princess Augusta, thought it a pious duty to keep up the traditional enmity with the boy's grandfather, George II, and friendly overtures on his part were firmly rebuffed. In the end, the King gave the boy up, remarking that he was 'fit for nothing but to read the Bible to his mother'. This was a pity as George would have benefited by going to court and mixing with a wider circle; but – prompted by his mother – he was always deeply suspicious of the old King.

Changes were made in the arrangements for the boys' education after their father's death, and for the most part they were for the worse. Except for George Scott, the old tutors were dismissed and new ones appointed. They were ineffective, unimpressive men who soon began quarrelling among themselves, demanding each other's dismissal and recklessly flinging accusations at each other of favouring the Jacobite cause. Two of them eventually resigned, and Earl Waldegrave and the Bishop of Peterborough were appointed to replace them. Waldegrave was far from welcoming the appointment and said he would have refused it, if he had dared, on the grounds that he was 'too young to govern and too old to be governed'.

He took it on, however, and probably did his best although he did not particularly like George. He thought him 'insipid', but by no means stupid, for his abilities, he said, were 'tolerable'; it was his pupil's character that troubled him. He did not deny that George was honest and that his religious beliefs were sincere, but there was something rather smug about him. He was inclined to pay 'too much attention to the sins of his neighbours'. He was not a boy to do wrong deliberately, but he was very obstinate in holding to an opinion – obstinate, too, in nursing grievances. He did not have outbursts of temper, but when crossed he turned sullen and silent. Above all, he was 'uncommonly indolent' – a fault George readily admitted in later years.

George's education had suffered as a result of all these changes, and the Princess Dowager, to do her justice, was worried about it. She did not depend entirely on Bute for advice for she also consulted Bubb Dodington, a turncoat politician who had been on friendly terms with her husband. She confided in him that George's education had given her 'much pain'. His tutors, she feared, taught him little and chiefly followed their own diversions – indeed she thought his book-learning was probably 'small and useless'. Dodington remarked that books were not so important – he should learn the 'usages' of the world. She agreed that he ought to go more into the world and mix with men, but she thought all the 'young people of quality' so 'ill-educated and so very vicious' that there was literally nobody with whom she would wish George to associate. 'Such was the universal profligacy,' she said, that she thought the danger of corruption if George went into society to be far worse than the obvious disadvantages of being cloistered away at home.

So George was kept at home with his mother to grow up immature, inexperienced and full of prejudices. She knew very well that there was something wrong, and she often said she wished he was less childish; but at least he was honest and good-natured and by no means, she thought, a 'wild, dissipated boy'.

He certainly was not – he had no chance to be. He seems to have shown no resentment, however, at the extreme dullness of his life, nor at the constant presence of Lord Bute. On the contrary, he emulated his mother's feelings and carried them to extremes. He thought Lord Bute perfection, no less. He would follow his advice in everything, he declared, he would do all that he wanted, and strive only to please him. He called him his 'Dearest Friend' and told him what a 'valuable treasure you are to me' and 'what a pretty pickle I should be in . . . if I had not your sagacious counsels'. He even worried over the state of his hero's inside: 'I am sorry my Dearest Friend is so rummaged by his medicine.' Lord Bute had done more than replace George's dead father in his affections; he had become the object of infatuation.

It has been doubted whether the Princess Dowager and Lord Bute were lovers, but it seems probable that they were. The

Princess was only thirty-two years old at the time of her husband's death and Bute – attractive, handsome and attentive – was thirty-eight. If they were not lovers, they were certainly very indiscreet in giving the impression that they were. Horace Walpole said that he was 'as much convinced of the amorous connexion between Bute and the Princess Dowager' as if he had seen them together, and Nathaniel Wraxall thought that she behaved to him in a way that was certainly not 'compatible with strict propriety'. As for the general public, they had not a doubt in the world about what was going on between 'Sawney the Scot', as they called Lord Bute, and the Princess Dowager.

> *He busses and smacks her by night and by day*
> *So well does he please her, she never says nay.*

If George accepted the situation without question, and showed no resentment against his mother, his brother William felt very differently. He hated his mother, and on her side she seems to have had little affection for him. She made fun of him, and laughed at him and enjoyed making him look a fool. One day, when he relapsed into silence under this treatment, she asked him if he were sulking. 'No,' he replied. 'Thinking.' 'Thinking!' exclaimed his mother. 'And pray what are you thinking of?' 'I was thinking,' he said with deliberation, 'what I should feel if I had a son and made him as unhappy as you make me.'

George, far from being made unhappy by his mother, seems to have clung to her company. In 1756, when George was eighteen, his grandfather, the old King, offered him an independent establishment, but he refused it on the grounds that his mother's 'happiness depended upon their not being separated and anything so sensibly affecting his mother must prove extremely uneasy to him'.

So George continued to live his narrow, confined life until, inexperienced and immature, he came to the throne at the early age of twenty-two. 'What could be expected,' asked Horace Walpole, 'from a boy locked up from the converse of mankind, governed by a mother still more retired?'

II

The 'Boiling Youth'

George III, like most of his line, was a man of strong sexual feelings. Unlike them, however, he showed no desire for a succession of mistresses or a series of passionate entanglements. What he wanted was a solid, respectable marriage – to a good-looking girl if possible, of course. But marriage certainly, and soon. He had a 'daily increasing admiration of the fair sex', as he confessed to Lord Bute in a letter written when he was twenty-one, and he was having difficulty in keeping his feelings under control.

'You will plainly see,' he wrote, 'how strong a struggle there is between the boiling youth of twenty-one years and prudence.'

A marriage had been discussed for him before this with a princess of Brunswick – a girl so charming that the old King George II said he would have been glad to marry her himself if only he had been a bit younger. As it was, he was prepared to settle for having her as a grand-daughter-in-law. George's mother, however, the Princess Dowager, was bitterly against the match and misrepresented the girl to George so cruelly that he gave up all idea of marrying her. The Princess Dowager gave George's youth as her chief reason for opposing the match, but she was possessive and probably feared that a good-looking wife might win such a hold on him that she herself would lose her influence.

There have been stories that George had at least one illicit love affair in his youth, and may even have contracted a secret marriage with Hannah Lightfoot, a Quaker girl of great beauty. A family in Australia claims to have evidence of the marriage and to be descended from George and Hannah. Given George's character, however, and the tone of his correspondence with Lord Bute, it seems highly unlikely that there is any truth in the story. It is a fact, none the less, that he did fall seriously in love at least once before he came to the throne.

He first noticed Lady Sarah Lennox, a daughter of the Duke of Richmond and sister-in-law to Lord Holland, when she came to court in 1759. He was immediately attracted to her and his passion continued to grow. 'She is everything,' he told Lord Bute, 'I can form to myself lovely. I am daily grown unhappy, sleep has left me, which never was before interrupted by any reverse of fortune.' He longed above all things to marry her and he hoped that Lord Bute would consent to the match. 'I submit my happiness to you who are the best of friends,' he went on, 'whose friendship I value if possible above my love for the most charming of her sex.'

It was obvious that Lord Bute would have no difficulty in dealing with so modified a passion, and George, indeed, was resigned in advance.

'I esteem your friendship above every earthly joy,' he assured Lord Bute. 'Let me preserve your friendship, and tho' my heart should break, I shall have the reflexion in dying that I have not been altogether unworthy of the best of friends, tho' unfortunate in other things.'

George had anticipated disapproval and he got it. Lord Bute had no desire to see his protégé allied by marriage to his rival Lord Holland, and he called on George to remember who he was and to summon up all his resolution. Lady Sarah was not to be his bride.

George meekly resigned himself – or appeared to do so; but he still could not quite resist Lady Sarah. She, for her part, was only interested in Lord Newbattle, a notorious breaker of hearts, but her love of the moment.

In October 1760 the old King died and George III came to the throne. In the spring of the following year, at a time when possible German brides were already being canvassed for George,

Lady Sarah broke her leg out riding. The King was all concern and could scarcely be prevented from rushing to her side, while the heartless Lord Newbattle merely observed that it would do no great harm for 'her legs were ugly enough before'. Lord Holland, busily enlarging to the King on Sarah's courage and patience under affliction, was soon quite carried away by his sister-in-law's prospects of becoming a Queen. His hopes were increased when the King had a highly indiscreet conversation with Lady Susan Fox-Strangways, who was a close friend of Lady Sarah. He asked her whether she would not like to see a coronation. She said she would. But wouldn't it, persisted the King, be a much finer sight if there were a Queen. 'To be sure,' she said. He now became more specific.

'I have had a great many applications from abroad, but I don't like them,' he said. 'I have had none at home. I should like that better. . . . What do you think of your friend?' he went on. 'You know who I mean – don't you think her fittest?'

Lady Susan was too astonished to do more than echo his words. 'Think, Sir?'

'I think none so fit,' said the King firmly. He then got up and went across the room to Lady Sarah and told her to ask her friend what he had been saying.

Considering that the search for possible brides among the German princesses was still being actively pursued, the conversation was not only indiscreet, but deceitful. His only excuse must be that he was young and susceptible and Lady Sarah seems to have had some particular charm of manner or expression which made her almost irresistible. She was 'at the same time different from and prettier than any other girl I ever saw,' said Lord Holland.

Lady Sarah was now carefully drilled in how she was to play her part in captivating the King, but the careless girl made a mess of it. The King came quickly to her side the next time she appeared at court and asked her if she had seen her friend Lady Susan lately.

'Yes,' she said.

'Has she told you what I said to her?'

'Yes.'

'All?'

'Yes.'

'And what do you think of it?' asked the King.

'Nothing,' she replied crisply, giving him a cross look.

The King went away feeling considerably put out; but for her part she was still obsessed with Lord Newbattle who had told her he wanted to marry her, but had later written to say that it was all off and they must never meet again. She had spent the morning in tears.

Her family, disappointed but not down-hearted, continued to ply her with advice.

'I am to look him in the face with an earnest and good-humoured countenance,' she wrote gloomily to a friend. If he were to mention marriage she was 'allowed to mutter a little', provided the words 'astonished', 'surprised', 'understand' and 'meaning' were heard. 'What a task it is!' she went on. 'The very thought of it makes me sick in my stomach already.'

The summer of 1761 wore on and Lord Holland went for a holiday by the sea; but not Lady Sarah. She was left behind to complete her conquest of the King by displaying herself 'dressed in a fancied habit making hay' in a field past which the King was accustomed to ride. But still the King said nothing definite and by June Lady Sarah was becoming bored. 'I won't go jigitting for ever if I hear nothing, I can tell him,' she wrote to a friend.

This was not to be her fate. The search for an eligible German princess had now narrowed to one or two candidates, with Charlotte of Mecklenburg-Strelitz the favourite. In May, George declared he was prepared to 'fix here'; yet in June he was still paying marked attention to Lady Sarah. For instance, on Thursday 18 June he told her that if she had gone out of town, he would have been miserable. 'For God's sake,' he said, 'remember what I said to Lady Susan and believe I have the strongest attachment.' By this time, his representative had already arrived in Germany to make a formal request for the hand of Princess Charlotte.

'The hypocrite!' burst out Lady Sarah when she learnt the truth. 'I shall take care to show that I am not mortified. The thing I am most angry at is looking so like a fool!' But she shed no tears. 'I didn't cry over him, I assure you,' she wrote to a friend.

The truth was that she did not greatly care; in fact, she seemed far more upset by the death of a pet squirrel just afterwards. Lord Holland probably minded a great deal more, for he had still had no hint of what was in the wind when he was called to a meeting of the Council on 8 July, and there learnt that Princess Charlotte, and not his sister-in-law, was to be Queen.

George had behaved inexcusably and it was only by luck that he had not hurt Lady Sarah as well as humiliating her. In her first anger, she said that if he changed his mind and asked her to marry him she would certainly refuse, and in after years, with anger gone, she still felt the same. 'I *still* rejoice that I was never Queen,' she wrote when youth was long behind her, 'and so I shall to my life's end.'

The wedding of the King, however, was bound to be an ordeal for her, and it was debated whether she should be one of the bridesmaids, as her rank entitled her, or whether she should refuse. Lord Holland was in favour of acceptance. 'Well, Sal,' he said, 'you are the first virgin in England and you shall take your place in spite of them all as chief bridesmaid and the King shall behold your pretty face and repent.' It appears that this was exactly what he did, for his aunt, the Princess Amelia, remarked on his behaviour afterwards. 'Upon my word,' she said, 'my nephew has the most wonderful assurance; during the ceremony he never took his eyes from Lady Sarah, or cast them once upon his bride.'

The bride was nothing like so much worth looking at – in fact she had been reported rather dauntingly as 'sans de beaux traits'. She came from an obscure little duchy and had had no expectations of making a brilliant match. Indeed, she had had no expectation of making any match at all, for her older sister was still unmarried and tentative arrangements had been made for Princess Charlotte to enter a Protestant convent.

She was an unremarkable girl, who, once in her life, had done a remarkable thing. In 1760, when only sixteen years old, she wrote a letter to King Frederick of Prussia to congratulate him on his victory at the battle of Torgau. It is not known to what extent this letter was 'all her own work'; she had a governess, Mme Grabow, who was a highly educated woman and she may have had a hand in writing it. All the same, it was sent out in Charlotte's name and this in itself must have taken courage, for behind its polished phrases and impeccable sentiments, an attitude emerges which is certainly not flattering to Frederick.

The beginning is forthright. 'I am at a loss,' she writes, 'as to whether I should congratulate you or condole with you on your late victory.' It was hardly a conventional opening for what was nominally a letter of congratulation. The reason for her hesitation, she says, is that the splendour of his victory has meant desolation for Mecklenburg. A few years ago the land had been cultivated, the peasantry cheerful and contented, and the towns prosperous and gay. 'What an alteration from such a charming scene!' Even conquerors, she thinks, would weep at the hideous prospect which now presents itself. 'The whole country, my dear country, lies in waste; on all sides it is a scene of terror and despair. . . . The towns are inhabited only by old men, women and children except that here and there a soldier, no longer fit for service, sits at his door and displays his wounds. His little children gather round him, ask a history of every wound and grow into soldiers themselves'.

She is aware, she tells him, that it is perhaps unbecoming in one of her sex to interest herself in such matters – 'to feel for one's country, to lament the horror of war, or wish for the return of peace.' Perhaps she might more properly confine herself to the art of pleasing and to domestic matters; but she feels she must intercede for her 'unhappy people'. 'To you even women and children may complain, for your humanity leads you to give attention to the humblest petition and your power enables you to right even the most terrible of wrongs.'

There is a story that this letter was shown to George and that he at once exclaimed, 'This is the lady I shall choose for my wife!'; but it is unlikely to be true. Apart from anything else, a wife interested in politics would not have appealed to him at all. However, they did have many interests in common. She was interested in music and could perform rather well on the clavichord; she was well-read in history and had some knowledge of botany. She was reasonably well-educated altogether, speaking French with some fluency, well-grounded in theology and particularly skilful with her needle. A further recommendation was the fact that she was used to leading a dull, frugal and uneventful life in her quiet little duchy.

Her looks were the only real drawback and George may not have been sufficiently warned about what he was to expect, for he is said to have started and turned pale at the first sight of his bride. She was thin, dark and on the small side, with a nose 'something flat', according to Horace Walpole, and an unusually large mouth. Her one beauty seems to have been her hair which was a pleasant shade of brown. She looked lively and good-humoured enough, but judging by the reactions of the people who saw her (rather than by portraits which may have been flattering) the general effect was undeniably plain. Years later, her Chamberlain, Colonel Disbrowe, ungallantly remarked, 'I do think the *bloom* of her ugliness is going off.'

Charlotte herself had been philosophical about her lack of prospects. 'Who will take a poor little princess like me?' she used to say. But she soon accustomed herself to success and set about choosing her suite for the journey to England. One of the servants who was to accompany her, a man called Frederick Albert, was not at all anxious to go. She insisted. Moreover, she told him that he must marry first, and even selected his bride for him. She was to be a certain young woman with whose family he had been on intimate terms. He protested that no such marriage had ever been discussed or expected, that he did not *wish* to marry the girl, and that in any case she was below him in rank. Charlotte, recognizing no distinctions in rank so far down the social scale, thought this objection purely frivolous and pushed the marriage through. She then, apparently, lost interest in it for she took Frederick Albert with her to England without making any provision for his wife to join him there. It was two years before she was able to do so, and then it was through the generosity of friends, not through any action of the Queen.

Charlotte set off for England in some state, but a curious spirit of meanness rather spoilt the impression made on the journey, for none of the customary presents were given. Charlotte herself, however, was cheerful and friendly, and her spirits even managed to survive the dreadful nine days they had to spend at sea. Her servants and the two English Duchesses sent out to accompany her suffered agonies of sea-sickness; but not Charlotte. She sang, she chatted, she was gay – she even thumped out English tunes on the harpsichord so as to 'encourage her companions in their misery'.

At last, on 7 September 1761, they landed at Harwich, Charlotte by now a little tired, but still cheerful, her attendants prostrated. The two Duchesses – the Duchess of Ancaster and the Duchess of Hamilton – revived sufficiently to give her a little helpful advice. Might she perhaps, they suggested, curl her hair? She refused, saying that she thought her hair looked every bit as well as that of the ladies sent to meet her. They had already tried to give her tactful hints about the sort of dress which would be likely to please the King. 'Let him dress himself!' she exclaimed. 'I shall dress as I please.' They then warned her that the King liked to retire early to bed. 'I do not!' she replied with spirit. 'I have no wish to go to bed with the chickens.' But these early evidences of independence were soon to be crushed under the heaviness and monotony of life at the English court.

Her nerve began to waver as she came nearer to the capital, and at the sight of St James's Palace she positively turned pale. The Duchess of Hamilton was amused, but Charlotte turned on her saying, 'You may laugh. You have been married twice, but it is no joke to me.' The wedding was celebrated that same evening, 8 September, in St James's Chapel. Charlotte was by now thoroughly nervous and upset, but she went through the formalities with reasonable credit. Her dress, suitably splendid but rather over-whelming, increased her difficulties. It included an 'endless' mantle of velvet lined with ermine which was so heavy that it dragged down at her shoulders, carrying half her clothing with it.

'The specators knew as much of her upper half as the King himself,' commented Horace Walpole.

When the ceremony was over, the procession re-formed and after a short stay in the drawing-room where a large company was assembled, they passed on to the private rooms. Supper was now supposed to be served, but unfortunately it was not ready. Charlotte, once more self-possessed and good-natured, sat down at the harpsichord and played and sang to the guests while they waited.

These minor mismanagements of the wedding arrangements were as nothing to the near-chaos of the coronation. It was preceded by quarrelling, for Lord Talbot, the Lord Steward, had made preparations for the banquet on such a niggardly scale that no invitations had been issued to representatives of the citizens of London. He was told with some firmness that it was most unjust that the citizens should be expected to pay out £10,000 to give a dinner to the King, and then have none themselves, so seats were hastily provided for them.

On the day of the coronation it was discovered that not only the sword of state, but the state chairs for the King and Queen to sit on at the banquet, together with their canopies, had all been forgotten. The ceremony had to be put off for several hours while a hunt was made. The heralds, too, had made a muddle about the order of the procession, and the Duke of Newcastle was found in the Queen's 'convenience'. At last the King was driven to complain to the Earl Marshal, Lord Effingham. He replied that he could scarcely deny that all had not been quite as it should be. 'But I have taken care,' he went on encouragingly, 'that the *next* coronation shall be regulated in the exactest manner possible.' Fortunately George was delighted by this gaffe, roared with laughter and made the Earl repeat it several times.

Owing to all these delays at the start, it was growing dark by the time the ceremony was over, and since it had been decided that there were to be no illuminations at the Banqueting Hall until the King arrived, the effect there was by now distinctly gloomy. The royal party arrived, in fact, 'like a funeral, nothing being discernible but the plumes of the Knights of the Bath, which seemed the hearse'. As the King entered, all the candles were lit at once, but this sudden illumination, however dramatic in itself, served only to disclose a depressingly meagre spread. 'Instead of a profusion of geese,' commented the Duchess of Northumberland, 'there was not wherewithal to fill one's belly.'

Even now, with all the guests safely seated at table, the slap-stick element persisted. It was the duty of Lord Talbot, the Steward, to bring up the first course, and he had decided that it would be a gesture fitting to the occasion if he trained his horse to walk backwards from the hall, so as not to turn its rump on the royal party. Unfortunately the conscientious beast had learned its lesson so thoroughly that it insisted on entering backwards as well, 'a terrible indecorum', said Horace Walpole, 'but suitable to such Bartholomew-fair doings.'

George had made a good impression in his early days as King. He had seemed good-natured and the levée room, it was said, had lost entirely its 'air of the lion's den'. 'This young man don't stand in one spot with his eyes fixed royally on the ground, and dropping bits of German news. He walks about and speaks to everybody,' said Horace Walpole.

This approval did not long survive his marriage, and when George and his bride went to watch the Lord Mayor's procession that same year, they were virtually ignored. On the other hand, William Pitt, who had just resigned as Minister, was greeted with wild cheerings while Lord Bute, the King's cherished friend, was hooted, insulted and pelted with mud.

The private life of the royal couple, however, began reasonably well and they were soon on friendly, even affectionate, terms. Years later the Prince of Wales, the future George IV, remarked to one of his brothers how lucky their father had been in finding a wife 'whose disposition suited so perfectly with his own'. On her side the Queen, understandably delighted at having made so unexpectedly brilliant a marriage, must have been relieved to find that her husband, in addition to being a great match, was good-looking and kind into the bargain. They quickly settled down to a blameless domestic life which *should* have been an example to all and made them universally admired; it did not. They soon became very unpopular indeed.

III

The Dullest Court
in Europe

George was the one sober and virtuous member of a uniquely raffish family, and life at his court jogged on in an eminently respectable way. It might have made him popular with his subjects, but his faults were not endearing. First of all, he was said to be mean. His court, reputed to be the dullest in Europe, was 'extremely unfine', as Horace Walpole put it.

This showed in the sort of entertainments they gave. The Queen's first party, a dance at which there were no more than a dozen or so couples present, was described as a 'gingerbread affair'. The guests arrived at seven, and after dancing until after midnight, they were dismissed without having been given any refreshments whatsoever. It was evidently considered as much as anyone could expect to have the chance of dancing in the presence of royalty without being allowed to eat and drink as well. 'History,' said Horace Walpole of this entertainment, 'could never describe it and keep its countenance.'

Lord Talbot, who had been responsible for the cheese-paring arrangements for the coronation banquet, was now in charge of the staff of the royal household. Economy reigned. One of his first acts was to declare that in future no meals would be provided at the Palace for anybody other than their Majesties, the Maids of Honour and the chaplains. Everybody else was to be on board wages, and everybody went short. The Maids of Honour were soon full of complaints about the 'abridgement of their allowance for breakfast'.

Supplies for the royal table were laid in on a far from royal scale – no more than six bottles of wine were bought at one time, according to a French diplomat – and it was said that at Richmond economy was carried to such lengths that the 'Queen's *friseur*' waited at table.

The King would not have considered any of this a hardship, for he was naturally abstemious and took no interest in the pleasures of the table. He loved roast mutton but little else. 'A leg of mutton and his wife, were the chief pleasures of his life,' wrote the satirist Peter Pindar. The royal food was plain and dull, and by the standards of the day, George drank very little wine – 'no more than four glasses for dinner'.

Apart from lack of interest in food, he had another reason for being sparing in what he ate, for he was terrified of growing fat. He considered this a 'real fault of his constitution', and once, when he was congratulated on his self-control, he said ' 'Tis no virtue. I only prefer eating plain and little to growing diseased and infirm.' It was also one of the reasons why he took a great deal of exercise. His uncle, the Duke of Cumberland, who was grossly fat, once told George that exercise was no good and that he was sure to end up as fat as he was himself. 'For I take exercise,' he said, 'constant and severe.' In his opinion, something more was needed; 'I mean great renunciation and temperance.' It was advice that George was well capable of heeding, and he never grew so fat as other members of his family.

In the interests of economy, George III busied himself with the practical details of the royal housekeeping and himself set about preventing theft and waste in the kitchens. He demanded to know why the bills for fruit and vegetables were so large, and why fruit was not supplied from his own gardens. He was told that the royal fruit was not yet ripe. 'Then let me not see any more at my table,' he said, 'until my own gardens will produce it in perfection, and then let me have the privilege, which every gentleman in the kingdom enjoys, of partaking of my own instead of buying from others.'

The royal greengrocers, a Mr and Mrs Miller, were blamed for their high prices and told they were no longer to supply the royal household. Mr Miller was able to prove that his prices, far from being excessive, were rather lower than they might have been considering the distances he had to cover in making deliveries, but George was adamant. In any case, he told them, all these luxuries were to be dispensed with in the future. Mr Miller seems to have taken the affair so much to heart that he 'shortly put an end to his existence'.

The aristocracy soon began to avoid the Court and all its threadbare functions, but others had no choice. Cabinet Ministers were often obliged to attend the King, but found that they could expect no refreshment to be offered them and they had to eat at a local inn. Professional entertainers fared, on the whole, no better.

George loved the theatre – it was one of his chief pleasures and he went regularly once a week for most of his life. He liked slapstick and pantomime best, and the sight of Jollett, the clown, swallowing a carrot five yards long gave him particular pleasure. He cared rather less for Shakespeare – 'sad stuff', he told Fanny Burney. 'Oh, I know it's not to be said, but it's true. Only it's Shakespeare and nobody dare abuse him. . . . One should be stoned for saying so.'

All the same, his interest in plays and acting was genuine and he liked to exercise his royal prerogative of inviting the great performers of the day to come to the palace and entertain the court. He invited, among others, Mrs Siddons, Kemble, and the celebrated Madame Mara. Mrs Siddons was his favourite. 'I am an enthusiast for her,' he declared, 'quite an enthusiast. I think there was never any player in my time so excellent, not even Garrick himself. I own it!' Mrs Siddons may have had mixed feelings about the royal enthusiasm, for it seems that she and the other artists were seldom paid for their services, or even given supper.

Good God! How kings and queens a song adore!
With what delight they order an encore!
When that same song encor'd, for nothing flows.

[31]

This Madame Mara to her sorrow knows.
To Windsor oft, and eke to Kew,
The royal mandate Mara drew.
No cheering drop the dame was asked to sip —
No bread was offered to her quivering lip,
Though faint she was not suffered to sit down —
Such was the goodness — grandeur of the crown.

And as for a fee — 'not a groat,' added Peter Pindar.

No doubt he exaggerated, no doubt he was often inaccurate, but there was generally a basis of fact for what he wrote. George himself, of course, may not have known whether the artists were paid or not, nor how much; but the image of a miserly king had enough fact behind it to stick, and it was not agreeable.

The public at large might perhaps have been more inclined to take a gay spendthrift King to their hearts, but George was no spendthrift, and he was not gay. He had his pleasures, but he took them in a serious and conscientious spirit. For music he had a genuine love and he could play quite creditably on at least three instruments himself. He liked religious music best, and made himself unpopular with the boys of Eton by making them sit through long concerts of church music without even the consolation of supper afterwards. In the Chapel Royal, he would beat time enthusiastically with his music roll and thump the heads of the pages with it if they began chatting among themselves.

Apart from music, his interest in the arts was conscientious rather than inspired. In painting, he much preferred the work of Benjamin West to that of Reynolds, and when confronted with the drawings of Blake, he would only say, 'What — what — what! Take them away, take them away!' But he did found the Royal Academy and dutifully walked round the exhibitions held there, making what he felt to be suitable remarks from time to time, such as, 'Clever artist!' 'Promising young man this!' With his favourite Benjamin West, he would even condescend to talk at length, allowing his 'kingly dignity to lose itself in long and familiar chit-chat'.

1a. The Scotch Broomstick and the Female Besom, caricature of Lord Bute and the Princess Dowager by George Townshend, 1762.

2. (overleaf) George III by Gainsborough.

1b. The third Earl of Bute by Reynolds.

The royal favour, however, for a painter as for an actor, had its drawbacks. Thomas Lawrence, for instance, was allowed the honour of painting the Queen's portrait, but he ran into difficulties from the start. First of all, she insisted on wearing a dove-coloured dress which made her sallow complexion even sallower. Hoping to introduce a little animation into his subject, Lawrence asked the Queen to converse with the Princesses, but this request was ignored as 'insolence'. Labouring under these handicaps, Lawrence produced a portrait which their Majesties considered unsuccessful, so they refused to pay him. Representations were made to the King, but he would not give way. If the artist, he said, would have the work engraved, he would pay his fee, but not otherwise. Since Lawrence could not afford the work of engraving, he never got anything at all.

Writers did, perhaps, receive a little more encouragement, but the King's taste was unreliable. He used to read aloud to the Queen from the English poets and he could claim to be a connoisseur of sermons, but although he saw to it that the royal libraries were kept up, it seems improbable that his interest in literature was very profound. It was in his library that he once arranged to meet Dr Johnson and won his heart for ever by according him a few minutes of royal chat. 'Sir, they may talk of the king as they will, but he is the finest gentleman I have ever seen,' declared Dr Johnson. In return, the King gave him a pension.

On the whole, George was more at home with the sciences and with handicrafts. He liked to use his hands and early acquired a dubious notoriety as the royal 'button-maker'; he is said to have turned a set of ivory buttons on a lathe. He really loved clocks and collected them, and he was fascinated by telescopes. He used to ask the astronomer Dr Herschel to come to him at Windsor whenever there was anything of particular interest to observe in the sky. A ten-foot telescope was kept permanently in readiness.

George loved to make drawings of maps and buildings, and he was a positive mine of detailed and pedantically exact information about all to do with military uniforms. He could reel off lists of facings, froggings, tags, laces, number of buttons, pigtails and gaiters; but his true love was farming. 'Farming George'; it was a nickname he deserved and was far from resenting.

He might well have been a success as a professional farmer – hard-working, conscientious, a little plodding, perhaps, but always quite ready to take an interest in new methods. Even as King, he found time to send letters on agricultural subjects to the 'Annals of Agriculture' under the pseudonym 'Ralph Robinson'. He saw to it that his sons were taught practical farming and both the Prince of Wales and the Duke of York had to learn to grow grain and to reap it. He himself sent his produce to market and sold it at a profit, thereby earning a good deal of unpopularity, for his subjects did not care for a King who competed with them at their own trades.

The trouble was, he was not nearly so good at his own, thrust on him by birth. Yet he was determined to practise it and not hand over all responsibility to his ministers, as he believed, perhaps wrongly, that his Hanoverian predecessors had done. He wanted to be active in affairs and exercise his full prerogative as King, but he lacked the intellectual resources and the knowledge of the world to make a statesman. Instead, he pulled strings, paid out money, and used his influence to get his way. It was one of his peculiarities that he was always utterly convinced that his way was the one right way.

He probably enjoyed these early years of his reign, pursuing his hobbies, chivvying his ministers and pottering about at Windsor, endlessly curious and never hesitating to poke his head into anybody's house to see what was going on inside. He wanted to know everything – how they managed this, what was the purpose of that, and, of course, how the apple got inside the dumpling (a perfectly reasonable question from a King unaccustomed to kitchens). The cottagers put up with the strange gentleman who asked so many questions, quite often not knowing who he was, but pleased when his questions resulted in the present of a new jack to cook with, a parcel of clothing, and sometimes money.

Good nature of this kind was a genuine feature of his character.

When the elderly Mrs Delany was left badly off, the King not only gave her a house at Windsor, but the money to maintain it, 'and to prevent even the *appearance* of a pension,' she wrote, 'the Queen used regularly to bring me the half year's amount in a pocket book when she made me a visit.' She was told that when she moved into the house she was to bring nothing at all with her as 'stores of everything would be laid in'. She paid, of course, for all this kindness by being at the mercy of constant 'popping in' by the King and Queen – an exhausting business for an old lady.

The King's good nature extended even to the acceptance of criticism on occasion. One of his pages once told the King that his royal father had been 'devoid of principle' and had ruined many people round about by not paying his debts, and that his grandfather, George II, had been as bad. The King's only comment on this piece of impertinence was to say that 'all this was rather too much to tell a Sovereign – although it might be, and no doubt was, true'.

Of all his pleasures, riding was his favourite, and he could never have enough of it. Accompanied by his long-suffering equerries, he would go out in all weathers, and often all day, at last bringing his companions and their horses home in a state of total exhaustion. He rode at least one horse to death. His equerry, Colonel Goldsworthy, spoke bitterly to Fanny Burney of a day's hunting with the King:

'After all the labours of the chase, all the riding, the trotting, the galloping, the leaping; after being wet through overhead and soused through under feet, and popped into ditches and jerked over gates . . . after all this, fagging away like mad from eight in the morning to five or six in the afternoon, home we come, looking like so many drowned rats, with not a dry thread about us – and then after all this, what do you think follows? "Here, Goldsworthy," cries his Majesty. . . . "Sir," says I, smiling agreeably, with the rheumatism just creeping all over me! . . . "Here, Goldsworthy, I say," he cries, "will you have a little barley water?" Barley water in such a plight as that! Fine compensation for a wet jacket truly! . . . Barley water after a whole day's hard hunting! And there it was, standing ready in a jug, fit for a sick room.'

It is an anecdote that crystallises the whole flavour of the court; kindly, frugal, prim and dull. If the King enjoyed himself, it is unlikely that many others did. The pleasures were mild and often uncomfortable. In the evening, music was played, but the equerries – and almost all the people at court but a privileged few – had to stand bolt upright, fighting off sleep and struggling for decorum. To sneeze or cough in the royal presence was considered unseemly – indeed quite 'out of the question', according to Fanny Burney. A sneeze had to be fought off at any cost, and if the struggle to suppress it resulted in breaking a blood vessel, 'you must break the blood vessel', she said, 'but *not sneeze*'. Absolute stillness was essential as well, so that if a 'black pin' unfortunately ran into your head, causing excruciating pain, the pain had to be endured without wincing; though if *very* great it was permissible, she conceded, to bite a piece out of your cheek for a little relief – so long, of course, as you did not spit it out. 'For *you must not spit!*'

While the members of the court endured, the privileged royal circle, generally including Mrs Delany, pursued their harmless avocations, generally drawing, sewing or knitting. The King would stride restlessly about, sometimes peeping in at the orchestra next door and demanding a favourite tune, sometimes making kindly, if dull, conversation, or else shooting off a shower of questions. Towards the end of the evening, he would permit himself the dizzy indulgence of a game of backgammon with one of his equerries.

By ten o'clock he often seemed to feel that dissipation had gone far enough, and the royal couple would make a move for bed. This was at an hour when, in more fashionable circles, the evening was scarcely beginning. It was the sort of quiet evening at home which the King enjoyed; but the Queen may have felt differently, for she is known to have quoted, on at least one occasion, the lines:

They ate, they drank, they slept, what then?
They slept, they ate, they drank again.

It is known too that she particularly enjoyed a game of cards, but one of the first acts of George's reign had been to reduce the number of tables at which play took place, and then to abolish it altogether for a time. He abolished Sunday 'Drawing-rooms', as he suspected they had a tendency to 'encourage a laxity of morals'. It seems unlikely. He also made a proclamation early in his reign for the 'encouragement of piety'. In it he prohibited all his 'loving subjects of what degree or quality soever' from playing on the Lord's day at dice, cards or any other game. They must 'decently and reverently' attend 'the worship of God on every Lord's day' on pain of his 'highest displeasure' and the 'utmost rigour that may be by law'. He himself was a regular church-goer and the only exception to his Sunday morning attendance was when he drove from London to Windsor on a Sunday to be on hand for stag-hunting the next morning. Dr Porteous, the Bishop of London, had the temerity to preach against this profane practice and George III was outraged. 'Porteous shall never be Archbishop of Canterbury!' he exclaimed.

It was not for the Queen to criticize the way she was now destined to spend her life. Whatever she may have felt, she said nothing; she betrayed nothing. She had once been a lively girl with some independence of spirit. 'I shall dress as I please,' she had said on the voyage over; and 'I shall not go to bed with the chickens.' But she did. High spirits were soon extinguished in the presence of a determined mother-in-law with strong views on how her son's wife was to behave, and a strait-laced husband, outwardly agreeable but endlessly stubborn and quite determined to have his own way in everything.

She had nobody to support her. She had brought only a tiny retinue from her own country consisting of her page Frederick Albert, whom she would scarcely have regarded as a companion, and two elderly women who were to hold the rank of personal servants. One of them, Mrs Schwellenberg, was the dragon who bullied Fanny Burney and made her years at court such a misery. Macaulay once described her as a 'hateful old toad-eater, as illiterate as a chambermaid, as proud as a whole German Chapter, rude, peevish, unable to bear solitude, unable to conduct herself with common decency in society'. This was the woman who succeeded in imposing her will on Charlotte to such a degree that nobody could come into the Queen's presence without her knowledge and permission.

It does not seem to have occurred to the Queen to resist; or she may not have wished to do so. Mrs Schwellenberg was, after all, her own countrywoman and her own servant. And she was company of a sort. For Charlotte must have been bitterly lonely during these early years. She had almost no companions at all beyond her servants, for the nobility avoided the court because of the drabness of the entertainment there, and the peeresses in particular, who should have been her companions, were not prepared to ask permission of a German servant in order to see the Queen. Her loneliness reached such a pitch that the King's brother, the Duke of Gloucester, wrote of her in later years that she had lived a 'miserably circumscribed' life. 'Except for the Ladies of the Bedchamber for half an hour a week in a funeral circle, she never had a soul to speak to but the King.' When Lady Charlotte Finch, her first child's nurse, came into her room, it was quite a 'little treat'.

If she had hoped to be translated from her tiny duchy into the gay life of a great court, she was cruelly cheated. She did mitigate the dullness of the royal meals by sending for smoked delicacies and her favourite sausages from Hanover, but she could do nothing but resign herself to the appalling cold and discomfort of the royal residences. 'There's enough wind in these passages,' said Colonel Goldsworthy, 'to carry a man of war.' And the cold in the Chapel at Windsor was lethal. 'The Princesses,' he said, 'used to it as they are, get regularly knocked up. . . . Off they drop, one by one: first the Queen deserts us, then Princess Elizabeth is done for; then Princess Royal begins coughing; then Princess Augusta gets the snuffles; and all the poor attendants . . . drop off one after another, like so many snuffs of candles. Till at last, dwindle, dwindle, dwindle – not a soul goes to the Chapel but the King, the parson and myself; and there we three freeze it out together.'

For Charlotte, the early years of her marriage must have been dominated by the endless, repetitive business of child-bearing which can have left her leisure for little else. She bore fifteen children in twenty-one years. Did she, like Queen Victoria, resent these pregnancies following so fast, one upon another? If so, she gave no sign. She lived her dull life, doing her duty, solitary and uncomplaining, seeing almost nobody outside the Palace but the King's mother, whom they visited with exemplary regularity every week. 'Are you going to suck?' the London crowds used to shout at the King as he drove by on his way to see her. They believed him to be ruled by his mother, and he was certainly an unusually dutiful son. He waited on her every evening at eight o'clock during her last illness, and towards the end, he and the Queen would arrive at seven o'clock, pretending they had mistaken the time.

She herself made no concessions to her illness, which was painful and protracted; she died of cancer of the throat. Indomitable to the end, she would order her carriage every day and drive about the streets in order to show that she was still alive. On the last night of her life, she maintained a conversation with her son and his wife for four hours, exactly as usual, though speech was difficult and painful to her. In the morning she was found to be dead.

George was, perhaps, incapable of deep feeling, and it is doubtful how much he really loved his mother, in spite of so much outward devotion. Mrs Thrale was greatly shocked to hear that all her effects had been sold at auction – 'even to her thimble'. 'I would not have sold my mother's thimble so,' she said. But whether George had really loved his mother or not, she had certainly exercised an unusual amount of influence over him in his early years.

She had had a lesser influence than Lord Bute, however,

George's idol for so long. Bute had been given high office early in the new king's reign, but it was not a success. He was hated by the people at large, who pelted his carriage whenever he appeared and daubed his walls with insulting slogans. Within a year, he had resigned. 'My health is every day impairing,' he wrote. 'A great relaxation of my bowels of many years standing is increasing on me continually.' He could not sleep, his health was tottering, he felt that he trod continually 'on the brink of a precipice – and this without even the hope of doing good'.

It was not the end of his influence over George, however, who continued to consult him for some time longer, but, as Bute himself had foreseen, marriage and fatherhood in time loosened the old ties. His 'dearest friend', whom he had once claimed to prize above his crown, was, in the end, discarded, and in later years George III was inclined to belittle the relationship which had existed between them.

At first, as the children came one after another in relentless succession, George seemed to be delighted with them and paid them great attention. 'I have never seen a more pleasing sight than the King's fondness for them,' wrote Mrs Delany. And just as he had busied himself with domestic arrangements and the way the kitchens were run, he now took a personal hand in the management of the nurseries. He was accustomed, so it was said, to place 'little or no reliance on the conduct of servants'. He would often appear in the nursery in the early morning 'to the no small perplexity and annoyance of those who had the charge of his children'. He 'thereby discovered many abuses'; and incidentally earned himself the nickname of 'Molly King'.

Both he and the Queen seem to have worried a good deal over the health of their children, who had to endure a number of unpleasant forms of medical treatment. They were confined indoors for long periods and for little reason, they were sometimes bled several times in a day, they were often blistered or dosed with strong emetics. They were vaccinated against smallpox, a hazardous procedure at that time, and Octavius is believed to have died of the after-effects. Their meals were as plain and unexciting as those of their parents and they only had two in a day. Their last meal was given them at two o'clock in the afternoon and they must often have gone to bed hungry.

The education of the boys was regarded as purely the concern of the King, but he did not make a success of it. Either he was badly advised in the choice of tutors, or he did not show enough personal interest in what was going on. The régime laid down for the princes was strict enough. The boys were up at six o'clock and lessons began at seven. They studied a wide range of subjects — Latin, French, German, Italian, mathematics and literature, religion, of course, and music. But they were high-spirited boys and difficult to control, and the King could never feel satisfied with their intellectual progress or their moral state. They were soon far too much for their tutors, and made nonsense of the narrow programme of entertainments laid down for them by the King.

The princesses fared rather better under the eye of the Queen. Their education was adequate, or perhaps more than adequate, and some of them showed flashes of talent beyond the ordinary; Elizabeth could draw unusually well, Sophia embroidered and was an excellent horsewoman, and Amelia had a strong feeling for music. Lady Charlotte Finch, a woman of intelligence and charm, was appointed head governess and Miss Goldsworthy, affectionately known as 'Goolly' and greatly loved by the whole family, was the sub-governess.

The Queen also saw to it that the princesses were well-mannered and considerate, and their behaviour was generally considered charming. She laid down that their governesses were never to 'pass any incivilities or lightness in their behaviour', and the princesses were also taught to devote themselves to charitable works. All the same, however much they may have owed to the upbringing of their mother, it was their father they loved. All through their lives, and in spite of everything which was to follow, they loved him dearly; but they constantly complained of their mother.

Charlotte lacked spontaneity in her relationship with her children, even in these early years, although in her relations with

[41]

the King there is evidence, both in her own letters and in the observation of others, of genuine affection. Mrs Harcourt, who knew the royal family well, thought that the Queen kept her daughters at 'too great a distance', and one of the ladies of the court even doubted whether she had ever possessed any real maternal feeling at all.

The strict rules of etiquette which both she and the King observed did, of course, make any normal and easy relationship with their children difficult. Even their sons, the princes, were not normally allowed to sit down in the royal presence, and as for conversation, nobody – not even his daughters – might speak to the King unless first spoken to.

These rules were naturally even more rigidly enforced outside the family, and they were sometimes carried to inhuman lengths. At the christening of Princess Charlotte, Lady Townsend, who was pregnant, began to show signs of exhaustion and the Queen was asked if she might be allowed to sit down. The Queen took a pinch of snuff and blowing it from her fingers said, 'She may stand, she may stand.' And the fundamentally kind-hearted King once kept his minister, William Pitt, standing in his presence for two hours, although he knew he was suffering from gout. Afterwards, he said that he did hope that Mr Pitt was none the worse for standing so long; but it does not seem to have occurred to him that he might have let him sit down.

Not only was nobody allowed to sit in the presence of the King or Queen, but if one or other of them came into a room, everybody in it had to back away until they came to rest against the wall. Ability to move backwards without tripping was something that had to be assiduously cultivated at court, as Fanny Burney bitterly remarked after catching her slipper in her train. 'No doubt,' she said, 'in course of time I shall arrive at all possible perfection in the true court retrograde motion.' In addition, if the King or Queen entered a room, all the occupants were trapped in it until they chose to leave, for it was absolutely forbidden to come between a royal personage and the door.

It seems a little ironical that in this setting the Queen felt able to complain of the difficulty she experienced in having any sustained conversation with her ladies. 'There is nothing she so much loves as conversation,' said Mrs Delany, 'and nothing she finds so hard to get.' She not only had to start the subjects of conversation, but entirely support them, as her ladies would only reply in 'mere monosyllables'. Apart from the favoured Mrs Delany, there was little else they could do.

In spite of the rigid correctness of life at court, it had none the less a slightly ridiculous aspect which appealed irresistibly to the gossip-writers and cartoonists. The King himself was a natural target with his gobbling manner of speech, his eternal 'What – what – what', and his rapid-fire questions. ('Thank God he answers them all himself,' said Dr Johnson.) The sort of stories which were leaked out of the palace delighted satirists. There was, for instance, the louse which appeared one day on the King's plate at dinner, and inspired Peter Pindar's 'Lousiad'.

> *The Louse I sing that from some head unknown,*
> *Yet born and educated near a throne,*
> *Dropp'd down – so willed the dread decree of Fate –*
> *With legs wide-sprawling on the Monarch's plate.*

The King calls for Mrs Schwellenberg.

> *O Swelly, Swelly, cried the furious King*
> *What! What a dirty, filthy, nasty thing!*

They examine the beast.

> *What! What! Hey! Hey! Now tell me, Swelly, pray*
> *Shan't I be right in't – What! What! Swelly, hey?*
> *Yes, yes, I'm sure on't, by the louse's looks,*
> *That he belonged to some one of the cooks.*

She advises action.

> *De barbers soon der nasty locks sal fall on,*
> *Nor leave one standing for a louse to crawl on.*

[43]

And it was all quite true. The King *did* give instructions that all the royal cooks were to have their heads shaved. One of them, however, a man called John Bear, refused and was sacked.

The Queen was outraged by the stream of lampoons and satirical verses which appeared in the Press, laughing and mocking at the royal family and the court. She could not understand how newspapers were allowed to print such things and she retired more and more into the secrecy and silence which was by now natural to her. This became more pronounced after the King's illness of 1765. It was given out at the time that he had a feverish chill, but it seems possible that he displayed some of the mental symptoms of his later illnesses. There is no decisive evidence of this either way, but it is certain that for the Queen it was a time of considerable strain. She was still very young and found herself virtually pushed out of the way by her mother-in-law, who proceeded to take entire charge. She was probably frightened and humiliated, and the whole experience may have undermined her confidence, even though later her influence over the King became far greater than that of the Princess Dowager.

Cocooned in the dull, constricted life of the court, weighed down by child-bearing and the growing claims of motherhood, the Queen made no complaint but fitted as best she could into the mould which had been cast for her. Perhaps she suffered; nobody knows. 'That little dear word silence,' she wrote in later life, 'has so often stood my friend in necessity that I make it my constant companion.' Behind the silence, perhaps a change was taking place so that by the time her daughters were grown up, all trace of her earlier liveliness and spontaneity was gone and they could only see her as harsh, bad-tempered and selfish.

IV

Scandals
and Royal Marriages

George, so unswervingly virtuous himself, was plagued throughout
life by a series of resounding scandals involving first of all his
brother and sisters, and later on his sons. Two of his sisters and
one brother died in their teens, too young to have got into serious
trouble, but his eldest sister, Augusta, although she was never
involved in actual scandal, was a problem from the start, always
ready to proclaim her disapproval of her brother's policies and her
devotion to his much-hated minister, William Pitt. It must have
been a relief to marry her off in 1764 to Prince Charles of Brunswick-Wolfenbüttel and get her out of England. The marriage,
however, was unhappy; her husband was coarse and brutal, he ill-
treated her and he was openly unfaithful. Of her first two children,
one was born insane and the other was blind from birth. Later she
became the mother of Caroline, the future wife of the Prince of
Wales, who, if not mentally unbalanced, was at the least eccentric
and provided endless scandal in the King's later years.

In 1764, the year of Augusta's marriage, the King may have
been hearing the first rumours of his brother William's attachment to Maria Waldegrave. 'The Duke of Gloucester,' wrote a
contemporary, 'has professed a passion for the Dowager Waldegrave. He is never from her elbow.' 'And what's more extraordinary,' said Lady Sarah Lennox, 'she *appears* to be in love with
him. I don't think it's possible to be so really.' This was a little
unkind.

Gloucester was only nineteen years old at the time, a dull boy, it is true, bullied and ridiculed by his mother as a child, but rather more serious-minded than most of his family. He certainly showed considerable steadiness in his devotion to Lady Waldegrave. She was several years older than he was, but a great beauty and a woman of character. She was the widow of Earl Waldegrave, and – less desirably from a social point of view – the natural daughter of a milliner, Mrs Clements, who had had a liaison with Edward Walpole, the brother of Horace Walpole.

George, even if he heard of his brother's passion for Lady Waldegrave, probably did not take it seriously at this time. He had plenty of other worries to distract him. In the following year his brother Frederick William died at the age of fifteen and another brother, the lively Edward, Duke of York, was becoming involved in a whole series of scandals. He was a young man of independent mind – he used to tell George that he lacked spirit in submitting so tamely to their mother – and he was also very highly sexed. He fell in love immoderately and often, and was sometimes taken rather more seriously than he intended. His life, however, was short, for in 1767 he put an end to his brother's embarrassments and his own existence by catching a 'putrid and irresistible fever' after a ball. He died in Monaco, showing, at the end, outstanding courage and resignation.

The rumours linking Gloucester and Maria Waldegrave soon gathered strength. 'He has given her five bracelets,' wrote Lady Sarah Lennox (now Bunbury) in 1766. 'That's not for nothing, surely?' It was not. Gloucester, by this time, was so seriously in love that Lady Waldegrave consulted Horace Walpole about how best she should act. He strongly advised her to give him up, so she wrote to Gloucester, on classic lines, saying that she was too good to be his mistress but not good enough to become his wife. They must part. In the event, they did the opposite. 'A short fortnight,' said Horace Walpole, 'baffled all my prudence.' The Prince began visiting her again with even greater assiduity than before, and soon they were behaving exactly like a married couple. This was, in fact, what they now were, for a secret marriage was performed in September 1766.

It was a well-kept secret, for although the truth may have been suspected – Horace Walpole certainly thought they were married and in consequence held himself carefully aloof – nobody knew for certain until six years later. The King probably had no suspicion at all for he treated Lady Waldegrave with great courtesy until he learnt of the marriage in 1772, when he immediately became hostile to her. Long before that, another brother, Henry, Duke of Cumberland, had been causing trouble. Cumberland had always been a 'lively lad' and had fretted against the frustrations of his upbringing. Once, as a child, he was asked if he had been confined indoors because of a cold. 'Confined!' he replied. 'That I am – and without any cold.' He was no more intelligent than his brothers – perhaps less so – and his education had been neglected. Horace Walpole dismissed him as of a 'babbling disposition' with a fancy for 'low company'. His most notorious love affair, however, was conducted in anything but low company, for in 1768 he fell violently, passionately and recklessly in love with Henrietta, the beautiful wife of Earl Grosvenor. He had no thought of resisting his passion, and scarcely any of concealing it; indeed such small efforts as they made to keep their affair a secret amounted to little more than token gestures. Lady Grosvenor would have her coach driven up Pall Mall under the Duke's windows, and if he did not happen to be looking out of them, up and down she would drive until he did. They were able to arrange a meeting-place above the shop of a Mrs Reda, a milliner, but it was far from private for she listened to their transports through the door and later gave embarrassingly explicit evidence in court.

'I very plainly heard the bed crack,' she said, 'and His Highness and Lady Grosvenor pushing very much; and I heard His Highness cry "He! he!" in a gruff manner, as if he was doing hard work . . . from this I expected I would find the bed much tumbled.' As she did; though not so tumbled, she said, as she had expected from the noises she had heard.

The Duke of Cumberland was in the Navy and so was obliged, from time to time, to join his ship at sea. This gave him an opportunity for long, high-flown and somewhat foolish letters to his beloved which delighted the public when they were later read out in court. Horace Walpole said the Prince's learning 'scarce exceeded that of a cabin boy' and that his letters were proof of it, but in fact they had a rather awe-inspiring fluency and reflected a genuine, if transitory, passion. In one letter, after giving prosaic details of the times at which he had dined, eaten his supper and gone to bed, he told Henrietta, 'I then prayed for you, my dearest love, kissed your dearest little hair and lay down and dreamt of you, had you on the dear little couch ten thousand times in my arms, kissing you and telling you how much I loved and adored you and you seemed pleased, but alas, when I woke I found it all delusion, nobody by me but myself at sea.'

He was soon back on land, however, and energetically creating fresh scandal. When Lady Grosvenor had to go to her husband's country estate, Eaton Hall in Cheshire, even Cumberland saw that he could not follow her quite openly. Now was the time, he decided, to make use of his talent for amateur theatricals (late fruits of his father's early training). He would follow her and they would meet at an inn every night, he appearing in the guise of a half-witted country squire travelling with a keeper called 'Farmer Trusty'. This character was to be played by Robert Giddings, Cumberland's gentleman-porter. Entering into the spirit of the part, the Duke arrayed himself in a variety of highly conspicuous disguises which attracted attention wherever he went.

At last the party arrived at Eaton Hall, still without open scandal, but once there, meetings were not so easy to contrive as in London; also they were now being watched. Earl Grosvenor had been warned in anonymous letters of his wife's indiscretions and he was determined to find out the truth.

The *dénouement* of the affair was even more undignified than what had gone before. On the journey back to London, Lady Grosvenor had arranged to stay at the White Hart in St Albans and Cumberland was to join her there, still in his character of the

3. Detail from the portrait of Queen Charlotte by Benjamin West showing the Royal children.

4. Princesses Charlotte, Augusta and Elizabeth by Gainsborough.

half-witted squire. The watchers allowed them to meet – this time in Henrietta's room – but at midnight, when the inn was quiet, Grosvenor's steward Matthew Stevens, accompanied by a groom, went to listen at the door. Two people could be heard talking inside. 'Now's the time!' said Stevens and flung open the door. Cumberland was surprised trying to struggle back into his clothes. He then ran off into the room next door where he proceeded to call on all to witness that he was not in Lady Grosvenor's room. 'No, you are not now,' said Stevens, 'but you was a minute ago.'

There was no defence possible when the case came to court – or at least none for the Duke of Cumberland. Lady Grosvenor was able to allege the dissolute behaviour of her husband as some excuse for her own conduct, but male peccadilloes were regarded as comparatively unimportant by the court when compared to any lapse at all on the part of a wife. Grosvenor's Counsel asked for £100,000 in damages against the Duke of Cumberland, but this was reduced and in the end, with expenses, Cumberland had to find £13,000. Of course he could not, and the bill was passed on to his brother the King, who could not have disapproved more heartily of the whole affair. He had to appeal to the Prime Minister, Lord North, on what he called a 'most private and delicate' subject. 'It regards the lawsuit,' he wrote. 'He (my brother) has taken no one step to raise the money and has now applied to me . . . I therefore promised to write to you though I saw great difficulty in your finding so large a sum as thirteen thousand pounds.' It was, of course, a very large sum indeed, given the value of money at that time.

Lord North, however, could find it, and did. The King was properly grateful.

'This takes a heavy load off me,' he wrote, 'though I cannot enough express how much I feel at being in the least concerned in an affair that my way of thinking has ever taught me to behold as highly improper; but I flatter myself the truths I have thought it incumbent to utter may be of some use in his future conduct.'

He flattered himself in vain, for Cumberland was scarcely out of one scrape before he was involved in the next. He abandoned

Lady Grosvenor to endure, without comfort from him, the scandal and humiliation of all the unseemly revelations brought out in court, and embarked on an intrigue with another married woman. She was the 'very handsome wife of a timber-merchant', and it was uncertain, commented Walpole, which was the more proud of the honour, the husband or the wife. Cumberland soon tired of her, however, and turned his attentions to a Mrs Horton, the daughter of Simon Luttrell, Lord Irnham, and the widow of Christopher Horton of Catton Hall, Derbyshire. She was good-looking, graceful and witty, and, above all, she had 'something so bewitching in her languishing eyes' that it was virtually impossible to resist her. Moreover, she had eyelashes 'a yard long'. 'Indeed eye-lashes a quarter of a yard shorter,' caustically observed Walpole, 'would have served to conquer such a head as she had turned.' Turn it she did. She used all her gifts, natural and acquired, with such resource and determination that the Duke had to marry her before she would allow him into her bed. He then lost his nerve and fled with her to Calais.

The King, on hearing what his brother had done, was outraged. The respectability of marriage was no consolation in his eyes for the disgrace of an alliance with a commoner. 'You fool! You blockhead! You villain!' he cried when at last Cumberland came to see him. 'You had better have debauched all the unmarried girls in England, you had better have committed adultery with all the married women! This woman *can* be nothing – she never shall be anything.'

There was nothing the King could do, however, beyond for-bidding his brother to appear at court. Cumberland was quite happy, in the meantime, living at Calais with his Duchess and giving balls under an assumed name. When he eventually returned to England, he was allowed to occupy his Lodge in the great park at Windsor, and to keep his equerries, but the King let it be known that anyone who visited the Duke and Duchess would not be welcome at court.

It was this marriage which led the King in 1772 to formulate the Royal Marriages Act, an outrageous piece of legislation which he forced through against the opposition of all the more generous-minded members of the Government. It laid down that none of the direct descendants of George II might marry before the age of twenty-five without the King's consent. After that, they could marry provided they gave a year's notice to the Privy Council and Parliament made no objection. Any marriage contracted in defiance of the Act would be invalid.

'I think it is the wickedest Act in the Statute Book,' wrote John Nicholls, a contemporary. 'It was brought forward to gratify the Queen's pride, to protect her from the mortification of having the Countess Dowager Waldegrave and Mrs Horton raised to the rank of her sisters-in-law. It was well said of some persons . . . that the title of the Bill should be "An Act to encourage fornication and adultery in the descendants of George II".' Even Pitt, now Lord Chatham, pronounced the Act 'newfangled and impudent', and the King was said to have no single servant in either House who would own the Bill; but he was determined to push it through. 'I expect every nerve to be strained to carry the Bill through,' he wrote to the Prime Minister, Lord North. 'I have a right to expect a hearty support from everyone in my service.' He ended with an overt threat. 'I shall remember defaulters.'

Gloucester, as soon as he heard of the proposed Act, came forward with the news of his own marriage, now six years old. The King was greatly upset and told Lord North 'my heart is wounded. I have ever loved him more with the fondness one bears to a child than a brother.' His older sister Augusta was almost equally disgusted by her brother's marriage. 'I long to know where these Dainty Widows are to be buried,' she wrote, surely looking rather far ahead. 'If it's by Princess Amelia [her aunt] she will make a great noise at the raising of the dead.' And it was not only marriage which Gloucester had to disclose to the King; there was a child on the way as well.

George made an effort to avoid taking any immediate action. There would be an inquiry, he said, after the birth, so that the authenticity of both could be established; but this did not satisfy Gloucester. Unless the inquiry were held immediately, he said, he would go to the Lords and state his case in person and in public. The threat was sufficient. An inquiry was held without delay and the validity of the marriage was officially acknowledged just two days before the birth of their child in May 1772.

In the meantime, Maria Waldegrave had written to her father, Edward Walpole, to give him his first news of her marriage. She had deeply regretted not being able to tell him at the time, she said, but the duty she owed to a husband was superior to that owing to a father. At the time of her marriage, she had promised Gloucester 'upon no consideration in the world to own it, *even to you*, without his permission, which permission I never had till yesterday'. Her concern was to 'secure' her 'character' without injuring his, and she had no intention of insisting on the title 'Duchess of Gloucester'. 'Very few people,' she wrote, 'will believe that a woman will refuse to be called princess if it is in her power. To have the power is my pride, and not using it in some measure pays the debt I owe the Duke for the honour he has done me.'

Horace Walpole was greatly struck by his niece's letter. 'How mean did my prudence appear,' he wrote, 'compared with hers, which was void of all personal considerations but her honour.'

Unfortunately the Duke's later behaviour did not match the genuine devotion of the earlier years of their marriage. He now began to be blatantly unfaithful to his wife and eventually devoted himself quite openly to Lady Almeria Carpenter. Maria was too spirited a woman to put up with such a situation and in 1787 she obtained a formal separation.

It was in the year 1772 that George's anxieties seemed to reach a climax. At the end of the year before, he had heard of Cumberland's marriage to Mrs Horton, and Gloucester, his favourite brother, had confessed his own marriage in February 1772, just as his mother, the Dowager Princess Augusta, lay dying. Worst of all, however, was the dreadful news that now came from Denmark of his sister Caroline's arrest and possible execution.

She was the youngest of the family, a fair, attractive-looking girl with a good deal of charm. She seems to have been luckier in her education than her brothers and sisters for she was said to be fluent in four languages besides her native English, to have some talent for music, and to be a remarkable horsewoman.

In 1766, when she was not yet sixteen, she was married to Christian VII of Denmark, a diminutive little man, quite good-looking and very nearly as young as she was. At the time, the fact that he was mentally unstable may not have become obvious, and his homosexual leanings were either not known to the English court or considered unimportant. His reputation, however, was already bad.

When the marriage was decided upon, Caroline Matilda wept. She wept because she was a child and she was to leave her home and her country and live among strangers. She wept and she wept — so much so that Sir Joshua Reynolds, who was to paint her portrait before she left, said that it was impossible to do her justice when she was always in tears.

She left England — still in tears. 'The poor Queen of Denmark!' wrote Mrs Thrale to her friend Mrs Carter. 'It is worse than dying; for die she must to all she has ever known. . . . May it please God to protect and instruct and comfort her, poor child as she is! They have just been telling me how bitterly she cried in the coach.'

Her husband, the King of Denmark, took an instant dislike to the grief-stricken child, and was unfaithful to her from the beginning. His stepmother, the Dowager Queen, disliked her with more reason, for she had wanted her own son to succeed to the throne. A wife for Christian, with children no doubt to follow, was as unwelcome as anything could be.

Two years after the marriage, King Christian decided to pay a visit to England, leaving his wife behind him. Horace Walpole saw him and thought him an 'insipid boy' who 'took notice of nothing, took pleasure in nothing' — except perhaps his own importance. 'He acts the king exceedingly, struts in the circle like a cock sparrow . . . and does the honours of himself very civilly.' But he did not deny him good looks, even though he was as 'diminutive as if he came out of a kernel in the fairy tales'.

By this time Christian was already becoming notorious for

the dissipated life he led, and whether for this or some other reason, he was not received with any show of enthusiasm by his brother-in-law, George III, who 'happened' to go to Richmond scarcely an hour before Christian arrived in London. Once there, he decided it was impossible for him to face the journey back again until the following day. Even then, there were delays about actually arranging a meeting and when it did take place, it was brief, George returning once more to Richmond and leaving his brother-in-law on his own; or rather, *not* on his own, for he had brought with him on his travels his constant companion, Count Holtke, a 'pert young gentleman' and Christian's current favourite.

Caroline Matilda, left at home, had begun to develop an independent spirit. In her husband's absence, the Russian minister treated her discourteously and she packed him off home. After Christian's return, she contrived the disgrace of the Prime Minister Bernsdorffe, who favoured Russia, and even managed to unseat her husband's favourite Holtke. It was about this time that she took to wearing men's clothes. Later, it became a common saying that she was 'the better man of the two', and when her mother, the Dowager Princess, came to visit her she greeted her at the frontier in regimental uniform with buckskin breeches. It was a costume far from becoming to her as she had by now grown extremely fat. When her mother expressed regret at the fall of Bernsdorffe, who had been regarded as a model of wisdom and fidelity, she merely replied, 'Pray, Madam, allow me to govern my own kingdom as I please.'

She was not far wrong in speaking of her 'own kingdom' for Christian's mental and physical health had begun to deteriorate rapidly, and he had become very dependent on a physician called Struensee, the son of a poor country clergyman. Chance had brought him into contact with the King, who had been at once attracted by him and had made him his Court Physician. Caroline Matilda was equally attracted, and it seems clear that they soon became lovers. This, however, did not lead to any breach with the King, for Christian had by now got over the antipathy he had felt for his wife when they first married, and was ready to regard both Caroline and Struensee with equal affection so long as they indulged him and treated him kindly. This they had the sense to do and Struensee soon found himself advanced to the position of Prime Minister and exercising almost absolute power; with the help, naturally, of the Queen.

They made a contented trio; but it could not last. Caroline Matilda was indiscreet and showed her attachment to Struensee much too openly, dancing with him whole evenings together at the court balls. Her reputation naturally suffered, and as for the upstart Struensee, he was heartily detested by the Danish nobility who were jealous of his power and influence. And in the wings was waiting the Dowager Queen Juliana, very much the Wicked Stepmother of fiction. She had always resented Christian as standing in the way of her own son's inheritance, and the more so now as Caroline Matilda had by this time borne two children — a son, to whom she was devoted, and a baby daughter. In fact, the care and interest which Struensee showed for her little son was one of the bonds between them.

The crisis came in January 1772. There was to be a masked ball on 16 January and the conspirators, headed by the Dowager Queen Juliana and her son Frederick, decided that it would provide a good opportunity to seize Caroline Matilda and Struensee. Count Rantzau, a general in the army and the head of one of the most powerful families in Denmark, had been induced to undertake the difficult task of persuading the King to sign an order for the arrest of Struensee and the Queen.

The King left the ball between twelve and one o'clock and retired to his apartments. The Queen stayed on longer, and after dancing with Struensee for almost the whole of the evening, she eventually left at about three o'clock. Rantzau had meanwhile stolen into the King's apartments, woken him up and told him that Struensee and the Queen had been plotting against him and that he would be in grave danger if he did not order their immediate arrest. The King was almost an imbecile by this time and he was physically frail, but none the less he had been fond of Struensee and was reconciled to his wife. He did not believe that they had plotted against him, and he refused to sign. In the end, it was necessary for Queen Juliana to take a hand before he could be persuaded. At last, reluctantly and with a bad grace, he signed the order for the arrests.

The arrest of Struensee was carried out without difficulty. Colonel Banner entered the room where Struensee lay asleep, followed by three officers with drawn swords. 'You are the King's prisoner,' he was told. Resistance was out of the question, his hands were bound and he was hurried down first of all to the guard-room, and then bundled into a coach and driven under guard to the citadel. Here he was put in fetters.

But the Queen had still to be arrested, and for this careful preparations had to be made. First, one of her women was sent into her room with instructions to tell her that there were some men outside demanding to see her in the King's name. She came out and found Rantzau in the ante-room. He handed her a paper signed by the King instructing her to remove herself to Kronborg, one of the royal palaces in the country. She guessed at once what was happening, but she showed no alarm and threw the paper on the ground. 'This is treachery,' she said, 'and could not have come from the King.' She demanded to see him at once.

The door of the ante-room was guarded by two soldiers, but she ordered them to let her pass. They fell on their knees, begging her to forgive them, but saying they must obey orders – they would lose their lives if they allowed her to escape. She stepped over their crossed muskets and they let go. She raced down the passages to the King's apartments, confident that she could persuade him to help her, if only she could reach him, but this move had been foreseen and the King had been taken to another part of the palace.

There was now nothing more she could do, and she had to allow herself to be driven to the fortress of Kronborg, about twenty-five miles away, where she was imprisoned in a cold, bare room, with no comforts of any kind. The only concession made to her was that she was allowed to take her baby daughter with her as she was nursing her herself.

The British envoy, Sir Robert Murray Keith, from this time onwards put up a spirited fight for her safety; he showed, in fact, considerably more concern than his master, the King of England. First of all, he demanded to see Caroline Matilda, and when this was refused, he said that undoubtedly England would declare war on Denmark if she suffered the smallest harm. He was afraid for her life.

In February, the examination of Struensee began. His nerve had failed, and from some confused idea that it might help his case, he blurted out a full confession of his love affair with the Queen, including the most intimate details, and even declaring that it was she who had pursued him and had overcome his reluctance. A special commission then went to see the Queen, hoping to obtain a similar confession from her. Keith had managed to send her a message, advising her to refuse to answer questions, but he had not known at the time of Struensee's confession, and neither, of course, had the Queen. When it was produced, she refused to believe it and said it was a forgery. There was no truth whatsoever in it. In that case, remarked one of her interrogators, 'there is no death cruel enough for this monster who has dared to compromise you'.

It was the one threat bound to be effective, for she loved Struensee utterly and absolutely, in spite of his betrayal, and she knew that if she persisted in saying that this confession was a lie, she would be condemning him to a hideous death. She was told that she might save his life if she confirmed his confession and signed a similar one of her own. She scarcely hesitated. 'Ah well! I will sign,' she said. By so doing, she had signed away her crown, her children, her reputation, and quite possibly her life; for infidelity to the 'king's bed' was, by Danish law, high treason.

She was brought before a special commission of thirty-five notables and on 24 March she was indicted. She was found guilty of adultery, and a divorce was pronounced in dramatic terms. The King, it was said, had no longer a consort, and there was no longer a Queen of Denmark. Caroline Matilda was informed of the verdict, but her first anxiety was for Struensee.

'What will become of him?' she asked. She was told that he would certainly be sentenced to death.

His trial began on 21 April, but the result was never in doubt; his confession had seen to that. His adultery with the Queen constituted high treason and the terrible sentence for treason was pronounced on him: his right hand was to be cut off while he was still alive, his head was then to be severed from his body and his body was to be quartered and exposed on a wheel. The sentence was carried out on 28 April, and was gleefully watched through a telescope by the Dowager Queen Juliana from her watch-tower in the Christianborg Palace. She is said to have remarked that the only thing that spoilt her pleasure was the fact that she could not see Caroline Matilda's corpse thrown into the death-cart as well.

Keith had been continuing his gallant fight to save Caroline Matilda, who was now threatened with imprisonment in the desolate fortress of Aalborg in Jutland. The news of her liaison with Struensee had naturally reached the English court long before this. Her mother, the Dowager Princess, had visited her in 1770 largely on purpose to warn her of the consequences of her indiscretions and to beg her to send Struensee away, and her brother, the Duke of Gloucester, had also visited her in the same year and for the same reason; neither had made any impression on her.

None the less the news of her arrest had still come as a shock, but the King disapproved of his sister's conduct so strongly that he could feel little sympathy for her. As for Queen Charlotte, she was outraged. She declared that she was ashamed to show her face in public. The Princess Dowager, near to death when the news came, none the less declared that Caroline Matilda's name was never to be mentioned in her presence again. She was no longer her daughter.

The result was a rather lukewarm response on the King's part to Keith's urgent despatches – in fact at first he seems to have taken no action at all. Public opinion in England, however, soon became roused on her behalf and the political writer 'Junius', in

a letter highly critical of the King, said, 'In private life the honour of a sister is deemed of infinite consequence to a brother. . . .
Is our pious monarch cast in a different mould from that of his
people?'

George III at last roused himself to write a rather tame letter to
his brother-in-law, the Danish King, asking that his sister should
be treated with fairness. Keith, however, continued to battle for
her liberty with resource and determination. He took advantage of
the dramatic statement which had been made to the foreign
ministers after the divorce, informing them that the King had no
longer a consort and Denmark no longer a Queen, to argue that in
that case Caroline Matilda had ceased to be a subject of Denmark.
She had become once more an English subject and had reverted
to the guardianship of her brother, the King of England. He
demanded her release. At the same time, he sent further urgent
despatches to England asking for more precise instructions, as he
could now only utter threats in very general terms. Matters were
becoming desperate, he insisted, for once Caroline Matilda were
sent away to Jutland, it would be difficult to secure her release,
and she herself was convinced that she would be assassinated.

At last George was galvanized into decisive action, in spite of
the cold disapproval of his wife. He submitted the papers concerning his sister's divorce to the law officers of the crown, and
when they told him that the evidence against her had been in-
conclusive, he sent firm instructions to Keith. If she were not
delivered up at once, he was to tell the Danish government that
war would be declared, and a fleet sent to bombard Copenhagen.

The ships were made ready in haste, but it was never necessary
for them to sail. The Danish government agreed to release Caroline Matilda, and in May two frigates and a sloop arrived to take
her away; but not to England. She had longed to come home and
live among her own people, but on this Queen Charlotte was
adamant. If she comes, she is reported to have said, then I go;
her mere presence in the country would be a contamination. It was
then suggested that she might go to her sister Augusta in Hanover,
but this, too, Charlotte opposed. Hanover would be far too gay,

she declared, for such an abandoned woman. So at last it was decided that she should go to the tiny Duchy of Celle and live in the Castle which had lain unoccupied since the death of Duke George William, the father of the unhappy Sophia Dorothea, wife of George I.

Caroline Matilda was not allowed to see her son before she left Denmark, and it was only after the most painful scenes that she could bring herself to part from her baby daughter; but she was thankful to escape into safety.

At this time she was still not twenty-one years old. Three years later she was dead. The cause was said to be a mysterious epidemic called 'military fever', or the 'purples', and its exact nature is not known. It has recently been suggested that it may have been porphyria, the disease from which, according to one theory, George III suffered; perhaps part of the truth may be that she did not cling to life, for she died, said the pastor who was at her bedside, 'like a tired wayfarer'.

It had been a harassing period for the King, and he must often have wondered why his brothers and sisters behaved so intemperately, and so very differently from himself; it was a thought which was soon to occur again, this time in relation to his sons.

V

Public Trials and
Private Dissension

There were other stresses and strains to be endured in these years, some of them in the sphere of public life, and it does seem probable that these may have played at least some part in George's later breakdown in health. On one occasion, when he was having difficulty with his ministers, he told Lord Bute that his mind was 'ulcer'd by the treatment it meets with from all around', and on another he burst out, 'See what treatment I receive from every set of ministers!'

It may or may not be true that George III's mother constantly exhorted him in childhood to 'be a king', but it is a fact that he interpreted his duties and rights in a rather more active sense than either of his two predecessors on the throne. 'I will not be dictated to by my ministers as my grandfather was,' he said. He may have been judging superficially, but there was no doubt about his own determination to rule.

George III was by no means the fool he has sometimes been made out to be, but he was both prejudiced and inexperienced, and was quite often wrong in the stands he took. Since he was always utterly convinced that he was *right*, and that opposition to his views must spring from wrong-headedness or outright malice, he was a difficult man for his ministers to manage.

On his side, he did not much care for them. Apart from his much-loved Lord Bute, who turned out anything but a success in office, he found the principal ministers of the early years of his reign distinctly unsympathetic. He could not endure William Pitt, who was in power when he came to the throne, and he had, apparently, no great respect for the Duke of Newcastle, who complained, 'I am the greatest cipher that ever walked at court. The young king is hardly civil to me, talks to me of nothing and scarcely answers me upon my own Treasury affairs.' Grenville the King frankly hated. 'I had rather see the devil in my closet than Grenville,' he said. He could not bear his 'endless harangues' and confided in Lord Bute that when Grenville had 'wearied' him for two hours, he would look at his watch to see if he might not 'tire me for one hour more'. Grafton was a relaxed, pleasure-loving man and an unwilling recruit to high office, but he got on reasonably well with the King, in spite of his reputation for loose-living. He had a mistress called Nancy Parsons to whom he was devoted, and he would let her take her place at the head of the table. 'Some do like it,' commented Lord Temple, 'some do not. She reproves his Grace for swearing and he, with great submission, begs her pardon for being so ill-bred before her.'

The King was genuinely sorry to lose the Duke of Grafton, but in his place he found a man who suited him to perfection. This was Lord North, who became Prime Minister and First Lord of the Treasury in 1770. He was an able, intelligent man, but lazy to a degree and always apt to nod off on unsuitable occasions. His physical appearance was unattractive, for he had coarse features, with a wide mouth, thick lips and great rolling eyes which gave him the appearance of a 'blind trumpeter'. But he was witty and good-natured, and through sheer indolence he was inclined to let the King have his way. Opposing him demanded a great deal of energy. 'My spirits, I thank Heaven, want no rousing,' said the King. 'Though none of my ministers stand by me, I cannot truckle.' Lord North, on the whole, did stand by him, for it was so much less trouble than standing against him. The fatal result of this compliance was seen in the loss of the American colonies.

George was for taxing them. Their defence in war had proved expensive, and he agreed with the party which argued that it was reasonable for them to make some contribution. The Stamp Act, by which tax was paid on all legal documents issued in the colonies, had been repealed against his wishes, and even the import duties levied at American ports had been abandoned, except for the duty on tea. The King felt that this tax was reasonable; they must pay something, he maintained, and in this view he probably had the support of a majority of the British people. Pitt, however, was against him. 'This kingdom has no right to lay a tax on the colonies,' he maintained, 'I rejoice that America has resisted.'

George – as usual – had no doubts about the rightness of his policy and he was confident of its success. After the 'Boston Tea Party' of 1773, when a mob of Americans flung the cargoes of some British ships into the harbour, he would not listen to the mildly conciliatory proposals of Lord North. He was for firm and vigorous action. Troops were to be sent to America to quell the rebellious spirit of the colonists. 'If we take the resolute part,' he wrote to the worried Lord North, 'they will undoubtedly be very meek.' Meek they were not. On the contrary, they reacted with anger, and prepared themselves to resist with all their strength. 'We have thrown a pebble at a mastiff,' said Horace Walpole, 'and are surprised it was not frightened.'

George was more than surprised – he was outraged; but even so, full of confidence. They were rebellious and ought to be punished, but he meant them no real harm, as he said later. He only intended to give them a 'few bloody noses and then make bows for the mutual happiness of our two countries'.

In the event, it turned out very differently, and by 1778 it was clear that there could be no hope of victory. The loss of the American colonies seemed inevitable and Pitt, now Lord Chatham, dragged himself to the House of Lords to protest against surrender.

'I am old and infirm,' he said, 'have one foot, more than one foot, in the grave. I am risen from my bed to stand up in the cause of my country.'

Nothing, however, could change the course of events. The war dragged on in misery and humiliation until final defeat had to be acknowledged. Lord North, for so long passive and acquiescent, was appalled when news of the final disaster reached him. He took it, it was said, like a 'bullet through his breast'. Pacing wildly up and down his room, he kept repeating, 'It is all over.' He sent his resignation to the King, who was furious at such lack of spirit – so angry, in fact, that he even made difficulties about allowing Lord North, his faithful minister of twelve years' standing, to receive the usual pension. 'Lord North is no friend of mine,' he said, with the vindictiveness he did occasionally show. It was pointed out to him that Lord North was not rich, and that whatever the King might feel about him, it would be a reflection on his own character if the pension was withheld. He gave way with reluctance. The loss of the American colonies was, for George III, an emotional and deeply-felt blow which he never forgot. Years later, he said, 'I that am born a gentleman shall never rest my head on my last pillow in peace and quiet as long as I remember the loss of my American colonies'.

This was the most serious defeat the King had to face in public affairs during these years, but minor frustrations were endless. It seemed intolerable to him that his ministers should not do what he wanted them to do without argument and trouble. To get his way, he had no scruples about encouraging his own friends to vote against his own ministers, and the exact degree of friendliness he displayed to his guests at his 'drawing-rooms' was liable to depend on the support they had given him in parliament. At the time of the Royal Marriages Act, he asked for a list of deserters of his cause for 'that would be a rule for my conduct in the drawing-room tomorrow.

He did not lack other means of getting his way, for he had vast powers of patronage; he was able to control promotion in the church and in the army, and to a large extent in the civil administration as well. He could give or take away valuable appointments at court, and bribes were almost certainly used on a large scale. None of this was out of line with the accepted standards of the day, but it did turn out expensive; so much so that in 1769 he had to ask Parliament to make up a deficit of £500,000 for him.

By 1777 he was again in financial difficulties, this time by an even larger sum. His servants had had no wages for over a year, and his tradesmen were on the verge of revolt. Yet still he fretted and fumed because in spite of all his trouble, in spite of so much money poured away, opposition persisted. He could not get his way as he wanted; perverse and wicked men, he thought, stood in his path and defied him. There was 'that devil Wilkes', a politician and journalist who had dared to call phrases in the King's speech false and misleading, and – even more impertinent – had actually criticized the size of the King's family. There was the rakish spendthrift Charles James Fox, making his brilliant, eloquent speeches, and not only criticizing the war in America but opposing an increase in the royal income. He found it unendurable, but however hard he fought, he could never get absolute control, and even had to face the humiliation of the House of Commons passing a motion in 1780 that 'the influence of the Crown has increased, is increasing, and ought to be diminished'.

In 1780 actual rioting took place in the capital; but this was a situation in which the King could show himself at his best. A measure had been passed to relieve Roman Catholics in Scotland of some of their disabilities under the law, but although mild in itself, it had influenced the somewhat unbalanced mind of Lord George Gordon, a fanatical Protestant. Raising ancient cries of 'No Popery', he led the London mob in an orgy of destruction and violence in which as many as seven hundred people are said to have been killed. Some members of Parliament had narrow escapes and the Bishop of Lincoln only saved his life by dressing himself up as a woman. Shops and houses were sacked and the furniture thrown into the street and set on fire. Fires, indeed, blazed everywhere and Newgate prison was enveloped in flames. The houses of the great were the favourite targets, however, and the mob broke into Sir George Savile's house in Leicester Square. Lord Mansfield's house in Bloomsbury was ransacked and then burnt, while he himself only just managed to escape by a back entrance. Lord North's house was also attacked, but was saved by a charge of the Light Horse.

For four days the mob seemed to have London at its mercy, and the King raged at the inactivity of the magistrates and his ministers. He sat up two nights running when it looked as though an attack would be launched against the Queen's house. On the first night he was upset because there was no straw for the troops to lie on, and he went to speak to them himself. 'My boys,' he said, 'my crown cannot purchase you straw tonight, but depend upon it, I have given orders that a sufficiency shall be here to-morrow forenoon. And as a substitute for the straw, my servants will instantly serve you with a good allowance of wine and spirits.'

On 7 June, he called a meeting of the Privy Council and asked for their opinion on what constituted a legal justification for firing on rioters. Was it necessary that the Riot Act should first be read out? They were cautious in the extreme, and gave indecisive and timid replies. None spoke up for vigorous action of any kind. The King then told them that if they were unable to give him advice, he would act without it, and himself lead a charge at the head of his troops. 'I lament the conduct of the magistrates,' he said, 'but I can answer for *one*,' (and he laid his hand on his breast) '*one* who will do his duty.'

He then sent for Wedderburn, the Attorney General, a man of a more decisive turn of mind, who at once gave the King the replies he had been wanting. If an assembly, he said, was engaged in an act of outrage which amounted to felony – and the burning and looting of houses certainly was such an act – then it was a clear duty and right to employ all means to stop the outrage. As to reading the Riot Act beforehand, it was unnecessary – and scarcely feasible – to read out that or any other piece of litera-ture to an infuriated mob.

While this consultation was going on, the Bank of England had been attacked, though unsuccessfully, several more buildings had been gutted and the prisons had been broken into. The King told Wedderburn to write an order to the Commander-in-Chief to call out troops and bring the situation under control. This they did amid scenes of horror and savagery. When they returned, their bayonets, it was said, were literally dripping with blood; but order had been restored to the capital.

Danger always brought out the best in George III. He was

threatened with assassination on more than one occasion, but he always met danger unmoved. 'I very well know,' he said, 'that considering the little care I take of my person, whoever chooses to sacrifice his own life may take away mine. I only hope, however, that whoever may attempt it may not do it in a barbarous or brutal manner.' One such attempt was made in 1786 by a mad woman called Margaret Nicholson, the daughter of a barber, who was convinced the crown was hers by right. She tried to stab him under cover of handing him a petition. He jumped back, but only just in time, for her knife had brushed his waistcoat. She was seized at once by the bystanders, but the King called out to them to do her no harm. 'The poor creature's mad,' he said. 'Don't hurt her! She hasn't hurt me.' He then gave orders that she was to be taken care of, before going on into the palace, where he gave the Queen the fright of her life by bursting into her room with cries of, 'Here I am! Safe and well, as you see! But I've narrowly escaped being stabbed.'

These occasional episodes of violence probably did little to upset a man as physically brave as George III, but the continual scandals surrounding his brothers and sisters, now rapidly succeeded by the even more outrageous scandals which had begun to gather round his older sons, were another matter. He had been a devoted father to all his children in succession when they had been small, but somehow or other relations deteriorated as they grew older. Perhaps a family of fifteen stretches paternal interest a little thin; or perhaps the primness and restrictions of his own early life, and the fact that he had been deprived, when he was young, of the companionship of people of his own age, made it difficult for him to sympathize with his sons as they grew into young men. He paid far too little attention to their education, he left them in the charge of unsuitable attendants and he seems chiefly to have hoped for the best. 'He [the Prince of Wales],' said Horace Walpole, 'issued from that palace of supposed purity, the Queen's house, as if he had been educated in a night cellar.'

The Prince had been much admired as a child. The London

mob used to hail him as a 'lusty, jolly young dog', and Mrs Papendiek, the wife of one of the royal pages, said that his 'countenance was of a sweetness and intelligence quite irresistible'. He and his next brother, Frederick, attended their father's drawing-rooms from the age of ten and developed social *savoir-faire*, if nothing else; but charm had always come naturally to the Prince of Wales.

Soon, however, the famous charm began to show signs of tarnish. As a boy, he had been merely high-spirited and mischievous. Once, when he had been shut out of his father's dressing-room for some reason, he had infuriated the King by shouting 'Wilkes and Liberty!' through the keyhole. He had never been a very truthful boy — as he admitted himself, he would always lie if it made life more agreeable — and the use he soon began to make of his remarkable gift for mimicry was sometimes unkind.

As he grew older, he began to mix with the wilder elements of society and he was often carried home to the palace dead drunk. In the drawing-room, he talked 'irreligiously and indecently'; but then it must have been a temptation to make *some* sort of a disturbance in those deadly evenings which dragged on interminably, with the Queen knitting, the ladies embroidering, the Princesses busy with their pencils, and the orchestra churning out 'all that fine squeaking', as Colonel Goldsworthy called it, next door.

The Prince's love affairs early began to cause the King anxiety, for he soon learnt to turn his 'irresistible' charm on women, showering his current fancy with passionate love letters, which would have appalled his father had he known of them. He begged a lock of hair from one woman of the court and offered in return a bracelet engraved with the date of his birth and the possibly compromising inscription, 'Gravé à jamais dans mon coeur'.

He and Frederick were given apartments in Buckingham House, as it was then called, when they were ten, and later they had their own little house at Kew. There were, of course, governors and tutors who *should* have kept them in order, but either they did not try or could not succeed. Mrs Papendiek says of two of the equerries — General Lake and Colonel Hulse — that they overlooked the domestic vices and irregularities of their charges when young. They did more – they almost certainly 'managed' the Prince's early love affair with Perdita Robinson, perhaps the first major passion of his life, by bringing her through the garden gate at the back of the house at Kew, and so into the Prince's apartments.

She was a woman of great beauty and some fame as an actress. She had other talents as well for she was the author of several works of fiction. including a tragedy called *The Sicilian Lover*, and she wrote verses for the *Morning Post* under the name of Tabitha Bramble. In the Park, she was a familiar sight, driving in a carriage preceded by outriders, her current admirers being recruited to fill this rôle.

The Prince, now eighteen years old, saw her playing Perdita in *A Winter's Tale*, and his heart was lost on the instant. Hastily dismissing his current love ('Adieu, adieu, adieu – toujours chère!') he sent off a miniature of himself to Mrs Robinson with another – and surely rather inapplicable – French inscription: 'Je ne change pas qu'en mourant'.

Letters of unbridled passion, hinting at, though not perhaps actually promising, marriage soon began to rain down on her. They also contained more concrete promises of money, and in particular huge sums he proposed to make over to her as soon as he was given his own establishment. How much reliance a woman of her experience can have placed on these promises must be doubtful, but she was certainly flattered – and very likely she was as conscious of his charm as everybody else. It must have been a blow to her when his passion, after a mere two years, began to show signs of cooling. By then, of course, it had become desperately important to the Prince to get possession of his compromising letters (carefully preserved by Mrs Robinson, whether for sentiment or gain). In the end, the King had to be called in to help, for the sums which would have to be paid out were far beyond anything the Prince could lay his hands on. The King found the whole affair deeply distasteful, though perhaps not altogether a surprise, for he had referred in a letter written not long before to the 'various rocks that surrounded every young man in this thoughtless and dissolute century'. Now one had shown up in the Prince's path and the King wrote a troubled letter to Lord North.

'My eldest son has got into a very improper connection with an actress and a woman of indifferent character.' A 'multitude of letters' had passed, and the Prince of Wales had made 'foolish promises'. The cost of purchasing the letters worked out at £5,000, 'undoubtedly an enormous sum,' said the King, 'but I wish to get my son out of his shameful scrape'.

He had shown a proper fatherly concern, but there was little of fatherly affection left by now. The two were on chronically bad terms, the Prince complaining that the King was always so 'excessively cross, ill-tempered and uncommonly grumpy', while the King could not understand his son's wish to escape from the dull domestic evenings at Court and 'dash into the wide world'. For the King, the Prince's celebrated charm had long ceased to work; but Perdita Robinson remembered it to the end of her days. 'The graces of his person, the irresistible sweetness of his smile . . . will be remembered by me till every vision of this changing scene should be forgotten,' she wrote.

The King was far more preoccupied with the Prince's demands on his purse. By the time he was twenty-one, he was already in debt to the tune of £29,000, but he could no longer be refused a proper establishment of his own. It was proposed that he should have £100,000 a year, which was not unreasonable by royal standards, but none the less this sum filled the King with 'utter indignation and astonishment', and he managed to get it reduced to a total of £62,000. The Prince behaved with good nature, but then he probably never had any intention of confining his expenditure within the limits of his allowance. He was thoroughly enjoying life – always 'in a dazzle', according to one of his sisters – and from this time onwards he plunged lightheartedly into debts which grew at an ever-increasing pace, but were not, on the whole, disreputable in origin. Some, of course, came from 'high living' – the traditional gambling, wine and women – but the greater part of the money was spent on a series of improvements to Carlton House, which had been made over to him, and later in building the Pavilion at Brighton. At the least, he was creating something.

The King, however, was shocked by his debts, by his way of life, by his unsuitable friends – the politician Charles James Fox, in particular – and most of all, his notorious love affairs. He even appeared to think that 'levity' might shorten the Prince's days.

Soon after the Prince came of age, he fell deeply and genuinely in love with Mrs Fitzherbert, a widow six years older than himself, who had been married twice. She was a woman of charm and high principles, and there would have been nothing to complain of, if only the Prince had not insisted that he wished to marry her. His intentions were inconveniently honourable from the start. The fact that she was a Catholic meant that if he married her, he would automatically forfeit his right to the throne; but of course the Royal Marriages Act made any such marriage illegal without the King's permission, and that would certainly not be forthcoming. He none the less pursued Mrs Fitzherbert with wild abandon and immoderate publicity. She loved him perhaps equally, but resisted his advances, until at last he made an attempt – dramatic, if not entirely serious – at stabbing himself for love. This had the effect of driving her abroad, where the Prince at once proposed to follow her, and when his father forbade it, he spent his time crying 'by the hour', rolling on the floor and tearing his hair.

At last she was persuaded to return, and they went through a ceremony of marriage in great secrecy on 15 December 1785. Both must have known that it was not valid, but both perhaps regarded it as a gesture of good faith – an earnest of what they would have liked to do had they been free. They were, at this time at least, happy in their relationship. Mrs Fitzherbert was described by Lady Charlotte Bury as a 'most faultless and honourable mistress'; but a sea of debts, now rising faster than ever, threatened to engulf them at any moment. At the time of their 'marriage', the Prince owed somewhere between £200,000 and £300,000, an almost inconceivable sum in those days, and he had no prospect of repaying it; unless, of course, he became King, or unless the King his father would come to the rescue.

The King his father was by no means inclined to do any such thing, outraged, harassed and indignant as he was by behaviour so alien to anything he had ever allowed himself. He would give his son money, he said, and set him on his feet again, if he married. (Naturally he knew nothing – or at any rate discounted – all rumours of any ceremony of marriage with Mrs Fitzherbert.) The Prince, frustrated and furious, said that in that case, he must retrench. He shut up Carlton House, he sacked his servants, and after selling his carriages and horses, he drove off to Brighton with Mrs Fitzherbert in a hired chaise, proclaiming that henceforward, though a Prince, he would do without even the normal perquisites of a gentleman.

It may have made a splendid gesture, and all the gossip and scandal certainly upset the King, but the rift between them went deeper. Some time later the Prince told Lord Malmesbury, 'The King hates me; he always did from seven years old.' He then produced letters to prove it which Lord Malmesbury described as 'harsh and severe; constantly refusing every request the Prince made and reprobating, in each of them, his extravagance and dissipated manner of living. They were void of every expression of parental kindness or affection.' Lord Brougham agreed. The King, he said, hated the Prince with a hatred 'scarcely betokening a sound mind'.

They were undoubtedly bad for each other. It scarcely seems to have crossed the King's mind that here was a lively, intelligent, not naturally vicious young man with no occupation to provide an outlet for his energies. He merely made the discovery, common to parents, that delightful little children grow up into difficult young men. He was not inclined to be sympathetic. He had been repressed in youth himself, and he saw no reason why his son should be more indulged. So he began to turn his affections towards his next son, Frederick, and nervously sent him away to Hanover lest he should be corrupted by his wicked elder brother.

Frederick had always been his father's favourite, and the decision to send him abroad must have caused the King some personal suffering; but anything was better than seeing his dear Frederick follow the evil paths of his older brother. Frederick left England when he was not yet eighteen years old, but the lessons he learnt in Hanover seem to have been the reverse of what the King had intended. He may have profited from his military training, but the lessons which really made an impression on him were those he received in drinking, gambling and sexual indulgence. The atmosphere was very different from that of the oppressively virtuous English court, and he threw himself into his new life with enthusiasm; he had always been an enthusiastic boy.

He came home six years later a changed character. He was still affectionate and he greeted his father and family warmly, but the one who at once became his inseparable companion was the one from whom his father had hoped to separate him – the Prince of Wales. They shared the same tastes and they exchanged lessons. 'The Prince,' said General Grant, 'has taught the Duke to *drink* in the most liberal and copious way.' (An unnecessary lesson, surely.) 'The Duke, in return, has been equally successful in teaching his brother to lose his money at all sorts of play – quinze, hazard etc.' The return of Frederick, to which the King had so much looked forward, in fact turned out to be merely an added worry.

The best thing he could think of to do with his next son, William, a good-natured, friendly boy, was to send him off to sea at the early age of thirteen. It turned out a rather more successful idea than Hanover. William took to the life of the sea with enthusiasm, playing rough practical jokes on his fellows and indulging in amorous adventures on shore, but always with amiable good nature. When he was given his first command, he rather unexpectedly showed himself a stern disciplinarian, putting his first lieutenant under close arrest because of a mix-up to do with the laundry. William wanted his men to be allowed to hang up their clothes to dry in the 'mizen rigging', but the lieutenant ordered them to be taken down. The dispute became a minor *cause célèbre*. William also issued irritating and complicated orders about shore leave, and went so far as to sentence a German artist, whom he had invited to live on board his ship, to a 'stinging dozen on that part of the body called the seat of honour', because of some disagreement between them. This proved expensive in damages. Nelson, however, thought well of the Prince; 'above all, he is a seaman,' he said, 'which you could hardly suppose.'

Their Lords of the Admiralty did not agree with this judgment, for although William may have required strict discipline on his own ship, he did not see why he should be subject to any discipline at all himself. On one occasion, he sailed his ship away from Antigua, quite without orders, and later sailed it home across the Atlantic, in flat contradiction of orders to winter in Quebec.

His father was unsympathetic to these youthful follies and was always giving William a 'set-down'. He did not like it. 'Fatherly admonitions at our time of life are unpleasant,' he later remarked. The admonitions had begun when he first went to sea.

'You are now launching into a scene of life where you may either prove an honour or disgrace to your family,' wrote the King. 'You should never lose sight of the certainty that every thought as well as action is known to the All-wise Dispenser of the Universe. . . . I strongly recommend the habitual reading of the Holy Scriptures.' On her side, the Queen exhorted him to 'shun low company, be humane and charitable to your inferiors. It was all very proper, no doubt, but hardly the sort of letter a small boy of thirteen, leaving home for the first time, hopes to receive from his parents.

Soon the King was worrying about expense. 'I cannot too strongly set before your eyes,' he wrote, 'that if you permit yourself to indulge every foolish idea, you must be wretched all your life, for with thirteen children, I can but with the greatest care make both ends meet and am not in a situation to be paying your debts.'

And of course William shared his older brothers' propensity for falling frequently and violently in love – in his case, too, with unsuitably honourable intentions. On one occasion he fell recklessly in love with a Miss Wynne, the daughter of an old broker in Plymouth. The father, in the 'foolishness and vanity of his heart', encouraged the Prince's suit, but the girl herself seems to have shown better sense. The King got wind of the affair and was instantly alarmed. 'Aye, what – what – what!' he is reported to have said. 'What – William playing the fool again? Send him off to America and forbid the return of the ship to Plymouth.' William shed actual tears of frustration; but off he had to go.

William was taken away from the Navy, which he genuinely loved, when he was only twenty-four years old, and condemned, like his brothers, to a life of futility and idleness. He managed, however, to remain on better terms with his parents than either the Prince of Wales or Frederick, for he was naturally kind; but his loyalties went instinctively to his brothers, and for a short time he joined them in their reckless London life. At bottom, however, his tastes were solidly domestic, if his alliances irregular, and on balance he probably caused his father less worry than any other of his sons, except, perhaps, Adolphus.

The King's deepest griefs in the first twenty-eight years of his reign, however, were caused by death, and not by scandal. The older members of his enormous family were outstandingly healthy and lively – the sons obstreperously so. By the time twelve children had been born, however, the blood was beginning to thin, and the Queen, no doubt, to tire. Alfred, the fourteenth child of the marriage, died in 1782, when he was only two years old, and the King must have been grieved by his death; yet in a letter he made the strangely cold remark, 'I am very sorry for Alfred, but if it had been Octavius, I should have died, too.'

One year later, Octavius did die. He was only four years old, and for a time his father was inconsolable. 'Heaven will be no Heaven to me if Octavius is not there,' he said. It was a grief which lasted his life.

Altogether, these years had been a period of much anxiety and a good deal of suffering for George III, but it had been caused by events and people outside himself; his own personal trials were still to come.

VI

'I Am Going To Be Mad'

In 1788 George III became seriously ill. His illness began, harmlessly enough, in June with what the King described as a 'pretty smart bilious attack'. It was unpleasant, his doctor was called in and he received the usual drastic treatments of the day; but the attack took rather longer than might have been expected to clear up. 'We have passed a full fortnight at Kew owing to the King's bilious attack,' wrote Queen Charlotte on 4 July. 'It is supposed that the dryness and heat of the season has occasioned these violent attacks.' But the affair was much more serious than that.

The King felt the need for a period of convalescence and a change of air, so he decided to accept the offer of Lord Fauconberg, one of his Lords of the Bedchamber, of the use of his house at Cheltenham. He had heard good reports of the waters, and the royal physician, Sir George Baker, approved of the plan. It was eventually decided that the King should spend some weeks there.

In July a small party set out early in the morning from Windsor; they were all up and about by five o'clock, and they completed the journey in one day. The party had to be small because Lord Fauconberg's house, Bay's Hill Lodge, had very little accommodation by royal standards. Fanny Burney, who was at this time one of the Queen's ladies and went with the party, exclaimed in horror when she saw the Queen's room. 'This, ma'am!' she cried, 'is *this* little room for your Majesty?' 'O, stay,' said the Queen, 'till you see your own before you call it little.'

The royal party was quite prepared to put up with the cramped lodgings, and they were charmed with Cheltenham, 'situated in a most sweet spot'. The King, in fact, was so full of enthusiasm that he insisted on taking the waters in unusually large quantities and said he was confident that, aided by 'good mutton' and plenty of exercise, he would soon become completely well. His day's programme was strenuous, and might have been found exhausting by a man in the best of health. He went to take the waters so early in the morning – six o'clock – that there was seldom anybody there. Afterwards, he went for a walk until eight-thirty, when he had breakfast. At ten o'clock, the carriages appeared and the party set off for a day's sightseeing – in this the King was indefatigable. Dinner was at four o'clock, and from six to seven o'clock there was more walking. After that, tea and conversation until ten o'clock when the royal party ate their supper. At eleven o'clock they went to bed.

It was not only a full day, but a long day, for if the King and Queen did not retire to their bedroom until eleven o'clock, they are unlikely to have been actually *in* bed before, say, eleven-thirty, at the earliest. At six next morning they were already at the Wells, drinking the waters, which must mean that they got up and dressed some time between five and five-thirty. At the most, they cannot have spent more than six hours in bed; on many nights, it must have been far less.

The King, however, was in high good humour. According to Fanny Burney, he had a 'flow of spirits quite unequalled'. It may have been the first small warning sign of the 'hurry and flurry' which was such a marked feature of his later illness.

His enthusiasm for sightseeing, and his apparent enjoyment of it, began to accelerate. He decided to pay a visit to his friend Bishop Hurd at Worcester, and here he became rather embarrassingly lively. On his second morning there, he was out and about at half past five and ran round to the lodgings where two of his equerries – Colonel Digby and Colonel Gwynn – were staying. He raced upstairs, shouted to them to join him, but before they had time to tumble out of bed and pull on their clothes 'as if surprised in camp by an enemy', he was off and away again. They had to run all over the town before they found him.

The King walked about the streets incognito, but he was generally recognized and followed by a crowd of admiring subjects. On one occasion, he came upon the bridge over the river, and turning to the people gathered round him, he said, 'This, I suppose, is Worcester New-bridge.' 'Yes, please Your Majesty,' said a cobbler. 'My boys, let's have a huzza!' cried the enthusiastic King, and set the example himself. 'A fine shout there was.' It was all endearing, but not a little strange. It led, of course, to gossip, and a rumour was started that at Cheltenham the King had run a race with a horse.

He wanted his servants to be as energetic as he was himself and he sent to London for bats and balls in case they should 'sicken for lack of exercise'. He himself kept up his busy round of visiting, looking at gaols, infirmaries, china manufactories, and a demonstration of cloth-making, which gave him particular pleasure.

He was very excited at the prospect of a visit from Frederick, Duke of York, his favourite son now back from Hanover. He was determined that he must be found lodgings close at hand, but there was no room at Bay's Hill Lodge itself. The King was not to be deterred, however, and he caused a small wooden house, which he had happened to notice on the outskirts of Cheltenham, to be taken up, removed entire, and then erected on a site just by Bay's Hill Lodge. The whole thing, involving considerable labour and ingenuity, was accomplished in five days and the house was ready and waiting just in time for his son's arrival.

It was wasted effort. The King was overjoyed to see Frederick, but the son seems to have been less enthusiastic about the prospect of a stay with his father. He declared that he could stay for only one night, because, so he said, he had to be in town on Sunday for 'military business'. The King was so obviously disappointed that Frederick had the grace to make the concession of travelling all Saturday night so as to have the whole day with his father. In fact, Frederick was probably hurrying back to London for no other reason than to rejoin his elder brother there. His leaving dismayed the King, but not Colonel Digby – the 'Mr Fairly' of Fanny Burney's diary. He disliked the violence of the Princes' 'animal spirits' and remarked that no amount of money would ever induce him to live with them. 'Their very voices,' he told Fanny Burney, had a 'loudness and force that wore him.'

Off went Frederick, and the round of walks, plays, concerts, and above all sightseeing was resumed. Fanny Burney wilted under the strain and developed a violent cold, which turned out to be influenza, while Colonel Digby succumbed to the gout and was let off his duties for a few days. But the King continued well and seemed to have benefited from his holiday. After they returned to Windsor in September, a concert and supper was given to celebrate the Princess Royal's birthday, and Lady Harcourt remarked that she had never seen the King 'in better health or spirits'. Yet he was not entirely himself. He suffered marked swings of mood – now irritable, now a little over-affectionate. There was an air of hurry about him. He changed arrangements and made new dispositions in his household perhaps a little arbitrarily and with insufficient reason. In general, he seemed eccentric; but then he had always given an impression of mild eccentricity with his rapid, stumbling speech, his 'What? What? What?' and his volleys of questions.

On 17 October 1788, early in the morning, the King sent for his physician Sir George Baker to attend him. He had had another 'smart bilious attack' and asked for opium to be brought to ease the pain. When Sir George arrived, he found the King still in bed and still suffering from acute pain in the pit of the stomach. He also had some difficulty in breathing and told Sir George that he had been having severe cramps at night and stiffness in the mornings. In addition he had had a rash, but this was almost gone. Princess Elizabeth had seen it a few days before, however, and had told Lady Harcourt that the skin was marked with 'great weals as if it had been scourged with cords'.

The attack was blamed on the fact that the King had got his stockings extremely wet the day before and had failed to change them before setting out on the journey from Kew to London. In the evening, he had eaten four large pears for his supper, and – perhaps as a result – spasms in his stomach and bowels had come on during the night.

Sir George Baker gave him strong purgatives, and when these only increased the pain, he prescribed laudanum. This, however, counteracted the effect of the previous medicines and he then had to be given purgatives all over again. 'An uncertainty as to his complaint is not very satisfactory,' recorded Fanny Burney. The King was better, however, next day, but worse on the day following, so that his return to Windsor had to be postponed. Fanny Burney noticed that the Queen was 'very uneasy'.

On 22 October, Sir George Baker was disconcerted to find himself received by the King in a 'very unusual manner'. 'The look of his eyes, the tone of his voice, every gesture and his whole deportment represented a person in a most furious passion of anger. One medicine had been too powerful, another had only teased him without effect. The importation of senna ought to be prohibited, and he would give orders that in future it should never be given to any of the royal family.' He harangued Sir George on this and similar topics for three hours.

Sir George confided these alarming symptoms to the Prime Minister, William Pitt the younger, and then hurried off to the Stock Exchange where he sold out all his holdings, thus producing a panic and a fall of ten per cent in share prices. Next day he confessed to the King, rather shamefacedly, what he had done, making the excuse that he had needed the cash for a very particular purpose. The King, by then decidedly better, made up his mind, with his usual conscientiousness, that he must make the effort to attend a levée on the following day, 24 October, which he had intended to cancel, so as to show himself in public and quiet fears for his health. His appearance, however, was more calculated to do the opposite.

None the less, on 25 October, just over a week from the time when his doctor had first been called in to see him, the King was thought sufficiently well to make the journey to Windsor. Yet he

5. Princess Elizabeth by Gainsborough.

6. Fanny Burney by E. F. Burney.

was certainly not in his normal health. His feet were still swollen and painful, his pulse was abnormally fast and his behaviour more than a little strange. Fanny Burney had a 'sort of conference' with him on that day – 'or rather,' she wrote, 'I was the object to whom he spoke, with a manner so uncommon, that a high fever alone could account for it: a rapidity, a hoarseness of voice, a volubility, an earnestness – a vehemence rather – it startled me inexpressibly.' And to Colonel Goldsworthy, the King said pathetically, 'I return to you a poor old man, weak in body and in mind'.

On the following day, Fanny Burney met him again as she was leaving the Queen. He stopped and talked about his health to her for nearly an hour, still with that 'extreme quickness of speech and manner that belongs to fever'. He complained of sleeplessness and told her that he had not slept 'one minute all night', but that otherwise he was well. There had, however, been a strange scene in the chapel that day. The King had suddenly started up from his pew, embraced his wife and daughters and then burst into tears. 'You know what it is to be nervous,' he said to Princess Elizabeth, 'but was you ever so bad as this?' She kept her head. 'Yes,' she said firmly.

His physical symptoms were still the same, or rather worse; his limbs were stiff and painful, and his incessant talking had made him hoarse. The Queen was becoming seriously alarmed and sent for Sir George Baker to come to Windsor. He found the King restless and over-talkative, but not incoherent, and he was still able to be moderately optimistic. 'He saw his way,' he said, and thought that all would come right in time. But there was no sign of it, for the King rapidly grew worse. The Queen, obviously under great strain, burst suddenly into tears when Fanny Burney was with her. 'How nervous I am!' she said. She had still no idea of how serious matters were and of how much cause she had to be 'nervous', for the King was still up and about, and able to go hunting, although he had to use a walking-stick when on foot. 'I could not,' he confessed, 'get on without it.' 'But the *Queen*,' he went on, 'is my physician and no man could have a better; she is my *Friend*, and no man *can* have a better.'

He was still amiable, still good-natured, but his eccentricities were becoming more obvious. The Duke of York visited him from time to time, and on 29 October he found the King in a 'violent degree of agitation'. It was on this same day that he complained to his doctor that his vision was affected; his hearing seems to have been affected as well, for he told Dr Ayrton, one of the Masters of the King's music, 'I fear, Sir, I shall not long be able to hear music; it seems to affect my head and it is with some difficulty that I hear it.' In addition, he had long had a particular fear of madness, and as his illness grew more serious this fear increased. 'I wish to God I might die,' he told his favourite son, Frederick, 'for I am going to be mad.'

There were ups and downs, and on some days the King seemed a little better. At least he was able to make some attempt to control himself, and he was perfectly aware that he talked too much. 'He would desire those about him to check him,' said Lady Harcourt, 'and propose that someone should read aloud to keep him quiet, but these means seldom obtained the desired effect.'

By 3 November, the King was decisively worse, and the Queen was desperate with anxiety. She spent most of the time sitting in absolute silence, with her hands and arms stretched across the table and her head resting on them. She could not eat, and 'silence and gloom' settled over the palace.

Dr Heberden, a distinguished physician who was now retired but who still had a considerable reputation, was called in to give a second opinion, although it was officially denied that the King was worse. In fact, he was still struggling for normality, and even managed to write a note to his Prime Minister. The note would convince him, he said, that he could still sign warrants without inconvenience and he was quite prepared to deal with a large number of them. He confessed, however, to a difficulty in reading despatches; but 'having gained so much' he went on bravely, 'the rest will soon follow.' He did not write to Pitt again for four months.

The crisis broke on 5 November. 'Oh, dreadful day!' wrote Fanny Burney. The King had gone for a drive in his chaise as he was no longer considered well enough to ride. He had seemed in high good humour, but gave so many orders to the postillions and kept getting in and out of the carriage so many times and with 'such agitation' that Fanny Burney began to fear that a 'great fever' was hanging over him.

As darkness fell, a 'stillness the most uncommon' reigned over the house. 'Nobody stirred, not a voice was heard.' The regular evening concert was cancelled and Colonel Goldsworthy joined Fanny Burney with a very gloomy air and hardly able to speak. A strange and deeply alarming scene had taken place at dinner. The Prince of Wales and the Duke of York had been dining with the King, when suddenly he began assuring the Duke of York that he loved him so much that he could refuse him nothing – except in so far as it might involve injury to the Prince of Wales. As for the Prince of Wales, he went on, he had behaved very badly to him, but he was still his son and he still loved him. The brothers preserved an embarrassed silence. Then the King lost all control and broke out into 'positive delirium'. The Queen had hysterics, the Princesses burst into tears and the Prince of Wales was so upset that Princess Elizabeth had to bathe his temples with Hungary water. Later the Prince of Wales claimed that his father had seized him by the collar and thrust him violently against the wall, half throttling him; but then he always had a taste for drama.

The Queen left the table and went to her room, followed by the King, who, though confused and incoherent and still talking incessantly, was full of solicitude for her. Lady Elizabeth Waldegrave, who was in attendance on the still hysterical Queen, made excuses for her by saying that she was ill. 'Then I,' said the King, 'shall take care of her myself.' He made up a place for her on one of the sofas, persuaded her to lie down on it, put out the lights and then kept hovering over her in a manner full of kindness, but so strange and unlike himself that the Queen was almost out of her mind with terror.

With difficulty the King was persuaded to allow her to sleep in a separate room that night, again on the grounds that she was not well, but he would only agree on condition that he should sleep in the adjoining room. It was midnight before he would let her go to bed. In the meantime, Sir George Baker had been sent for in a hurry and was alarmed to find unmistakeable signs that the King's mind was now affected. Sir George also found that his pulse was very fast, although he was unable to take it accurately for it was impossible to persuade the King to keep still for long enough.

The events of this terrifying night were still not over, for at one in the morning, as the Queen lay sleepless on her bed with Miss Goldsworthy – 'Goolly' – sitting beside her, the King suddenly came in. He had taken it into his head that the Queen might have been moved from the Palace, and he pulled back the bed-curtains and held a candle to her face. 'I will confess the truth,' he said, 'I thought you had deceived me and that you was not here.' The Queen was silent – she was too frightened to speak. 'Goolly,' went on the King, turning to Miss Goldsworthy, 'you are honest, I can depend upon you, you will take care of her. They said the King was ill, he was not ill, but now the Queen is ill, he is ill, too.'

At last the terrified Queen tried to persuade him to leave her and go to bed, but it was half an hour before he finally went, banging the door after him and locking it. She lay sleepless all night, terrified that he might return, and Fanny Burney was shocked by the state in which she found her next morning. She had, however, been given a warning by 'Mr Fairly' of what she might expect.

'How are you?' he had asked her. 'Are you strong? Are you stout? Can you go through such scenes as these? You do not look much fitted for them.'

Fanny Burney replied that she would do very well, for at such a time her only thought would be for the Queen. Her genuine concern did indeed lead her to do the one right thing when she went into the Queen's room. She ran to the Queen, tried to speak, failed, and then burst into tears. At this, the Queen wept, too – 'a perfect agony of weeping ensued, which, once begun, she could not stop'. When at last the Queen could collect herself, she said, 'It is a great relief to me. I had not been able to cry before, all this night long.'

The King was still in the next room with his two doctors, and his hoarse voice could be heard through the door, talking, talking, talking. The Queen asked Fanny Burney to listen at the door and tell her what he was saying. She could hear clearly enough. 'I am nervous,' the King kept on repeating. 'I am not ill, but I am nervous. If you would know what is the matter with me, I am nervous. But I love you both very well,' he assured his two doctors, ' – if you would tell me the truth. I love Dr Heberden best, for he has not told me a lie. Sir George has told me a lie – a white lie, he says, but I hate a white lie! If you will tell me a lie, let it be a black lie!'

The Queen asked Fanny Burney to stay at the door so as to warn her if it seemed that the King was about to come in. She dreaded seeing him. His appearance, even apart from his manner and wild talk, had alarmed her beyond words. His eyes, as she confided later to Lady Harcourt, looked like nothing so much as 'blackcurrant jelly', the veins of his face were all swollen and 'foam ran out of his mouth'.

Sir George Baker now asked that Dr Richard Warren, the Prince of Wales's doctor, should be sent for, in spite of the King's known dislike of him. Sir George said that he was far from well himself, and – a naturally timid man – he obviously felt that he could no longer cope with the responsibility of the King's illness with no help but that of the elderly Dr Heberden. The Prince of Wales agreed without asking the Queen, and the visit was arranged.

When he came, the Queen, though still in her nightclothes, naturally expected that Dr Warren would come and report to her and tell her what impression he had formed of the King's illness. She was told that the King had refused to see Dr Warren, but that Dr Warren had stationed himself in a place where he could listen to the King talking, and that he had consulted with Sir George Baker on the case. The Queen waited for further news. One of her ladies then reported that Dr Warren was no longer in the place where he had been standing, so the Queen, now weeping freely, prepared herself to receive him and to face whatever news he might bring. Still he did not come. Lady Elizabeth Walde-

[85]

grave then went out to make enquiries. She returned with the news that Dr Warren was gone. 'Run! Stop him!' cried the Queen. 'Let him but let me know what I am to do!' It was too late. Dr Warren had left the Queen's Lodge and had gone over to the Castle to report to the Prince of Wales. The Queen was superseded, and the Prince in entire charge.

Dr Warren was a physician who was very popular in the fashionable world as he had the knack of ingratiating himself with his patients. He would lend them money and was careful to prescribe for them what he knew they wanted – it might be a holiday abroad, or complete rest from irritating responsibilities, with a rich diet and plenty to drink. He probably felt able to make a guess at what the Prince of Wales wanted – he would want to be King in fact, if not in name. At all events, he gave an almost completely hopeless diagnosis. The King's life was in danger, and if he did live, it was unlikely that he would recover his reason.

The King, for his part, eventually received Dr Warren, but with great coldness. He told him, 'You may come here as an acquaintance, but not as *my* physician. No man can serve two masters. You are the Prince of Wales's physician, you cannot be mine.'

The Queen had been greatly shocked by the news that Dr Warren had left without seeing her on his first visit. 'I think a deeper blow I have never witnessed,' said Fanny Burney. 'Already to become but second, even for the King.' A quarter of an hour after he had left, however, Colonel Goldsworthy had arrived and asked for an audience. He had told the Queen that the physicians were unanimous in thinking that she should remove to an apartment further away from the King, since he would undoubtedly be harmed by the agitation which seeing her would cause, and there could be no possibility of preventing it while she remained so near at hand.

She agreed without resistance, but in a mood of bitter grief, and when she arrived in her new apartments, her control gave way. 'What will become of me? What will become of me?' she kept repeating. The Prince of Wales came over to see her a little later on. He was naturally kind-hearted and although he had been on bad terms with his parents for some time, he did his best to be sympathetic. It was later, perhaps due to the promptings of his Whig friends who hoped to gain power, that he began to appreciate the advantages to himself if his father should be permanently mad.

Yet even now, at this early stage, he showed a certain lack of sensitivity. His luncheon parties, held in a room directly below his mother's, tended to be gay and noisy. 'He's a glorious, jolly dog,' called out Dr Warren, emerging after a session of wine-drinking with the Prince. The Queen, sitting silent in her dressing-gown upstairs, scarcely eating or drinking at all, at last roused herself to tell the Prince that he must take his meals in the Castle. Otherwise, she seemed willing to hand over complete control into the Prince's hands. 'Nothing,' said Fanny Burney, 'was done but by his orders and he was applied to in every difficulty.' The Queen spent all her time in her new apartments, consisting of two rooms only, and never stirred outside them. Nor were people from the out-side world any longer admitted to her house, apart from a small number of attendants chosen by the Prince.

Sir George Baker, leaning gratefully on the stronger character of Dr Warren, accepted his gloomy prognosis and wrote off to in-form Pitt that the King's mental disturbance now persisted all day long and that there seemed little likelihood of an immediate change.

Rumours about the nature of the King's illness had by now be-gun to spread in society – it was impossible that it should be kept secret, for the political repercussions were obvious. William Gren-ville wrote to his brother the Marquis of Buckingham on 7 November to tell him that there seemed little chance that the King could recover both his 'health and his understanding', and that if the disturbance of mind continued, he might 'live years in this melancholy state; and this, of all events that can happen, is per-haps the most to be feared.'

The King's mood had now sunk into one of deep melancholy, and he would talk of his dead son Octavius, and grieve over his death till the tears ran down his face. 'I must have been very sinful,' he would say, 'to be so sorely chastened.' Lord North called to enquire one day, but the King would not receive him 'He, poor fellow, has lost his sight,' he said, 'and I my mind. Yet we meant well to the Americans. . . . Tell him not to call again – I shall never see him.'

He still had moments when he was rational, but the 'hurry and flurry' which had marked the early stages of his illness was now spinning out of control. In every popular sense of the word, he was 'mad'. Pitt summed up a report he had received from the Prince of Wales as indicating that it was quite out of the question for the King to carry out any business at the moment, and that 'on the whole, there was more ground to fear than to hope'.

The Prince's Comptroller of the Household, Captain Payne, a rather mischievous and unattractive character, was already full of excitement at the prospect of power for the Prince's party and was busy pulling all the political strings he could. He wrote off in high delight to the playwright and politician, Richard Brinsley Sheridan, who, with Fox and Burke, was one of the leaders of the Whig party. With no attempt at concealing his glee, he told him that the King was becoming worse all the time and that the doctors thought it unlikely that he would survive very long. The Archbishop, he said, had offered to attend the King, but had not been asked to come, 'it being thought too late'.

The King had indeed been very ill, and perhaps near to death, on 9 November, and again on the following day, when he suffered what may have been convulsions, followed by coma. He made a remarkable recovery physically, but it was feared that his brain was permanently damaged. Lord Bulkeley, who had been to Windsor to enquire, said in a letter to the Marquis of Buckingham, 'sorry am I to tell you that poor Rex's state seems worse than a thousand deaths'.

One of the King's equerries, Robert Fulke Greville (the 'Colonel Welbred' of Fanny Burney's diary), had hurried to Windsor as soon as he heard of the King's illness, and from early November he kept a day-by-day record of the King's state. He found him disturbed and rambling, suffering badly from insomnia, but still able to recognize people. On 11 November he wrote, 'I saw him this night sit up and eat his posset, and afterwards take his draught. The former he ate as well and seemingly as composed as ever, but the ramblings continued and were more wild than before, amounting alas to an almost total suspension of reason. No sleep this night. The talking incessant throughout.'

A decisive improvement occurred, however, on the night of 12 November. About a quarter to four the King became 'quite recollected' and asked for water to clean out his mouth. When it was brought, he 'did it as well as could be, washing his mouth and gargelling as well as ever in his usual habits'. He asked Greville how many days he had been confined to his bed, then 'looked round at his attendants with attention, and smiled and nodded to them frequently'. When day came, he seemed much more rational and composed than he had been for some time.

The King's condition, in fact, seemed to vary day by day, and almost hour by hour, but Dr Warren's pessimism did not vary, and, uninhibited by any ideas of professional secrecy, he spread the gloomiest reports among his high society patients. 'Rex noster insanit,' he informed Lady Spencer, the mother of the Prince's close friend, the Duchess of Devonshire. The hopes of the Prince's party rose higher than ever as the news spread; he might not be able to become King in name, but it looked as though he would rule.

At Windsor, the King still talked and talked. They did their best to keep him quiet, but with little success and he became increasingly exhausted and hoarse. 'His voice was every now and then interrupted by a catch in the throat,' said Robert Greville. On 19 November he talked for nineteen hours without stopping. But he still had his flashes of good sense. When Dr Warren told him that he really must stop talking, the King replied, 'I know that as well as you. It is my complaint. Cure me of that and I shall be well.'

The King would have been bound to suffer in any case as a result of his illness, but he also suffered at the hands of his physicians, who unflaggingly applied the heroic remedies of eighteenth-century medicine. At first he was thought to be suffering from the 'flying gout', that puzzling affliction of the period. It was thought that the gout, which had first attacked his feet, had flown to his brain and lodged there, so blisters were applied to his head in the hope of driving it down again. The blisters suppurated and became extremely painful. He was given violent purges which caused him severe discomfort, and the physicians refused to allow a fire in his room as they thought it increased his fever. His room, in fact, was kept so cold that his attendants could not endure staying in it for more than two hours at a time; but *he* had to stay there all day. His windows were now screwed up – a reasonable precaution if they thought him suicidal, but it was alarming and humiliating to the King. Worst of all, he was still not allowed to see his wife and his daughters. 'I know not what the physicians mean by their conduct,' wrote Mrs Harcourt; 'they seem to be amusing themselves . . . and feel no more for him than if he were a dog or a cat.'

He did what he could to show his resentment. He marked the names in the Court Circular of the people he intended to dismiss as soon as he was well. He refused to be shaved, he refused to eat his dinner. When at length he did consent to be shaved, he stopped the operation halfway through and demanded other indulgences. For some time he remained with only half of his face shaved, presenting a bizarre appearance, said Greville, as he had not been shaved for more than a fortnight. At last he give in; but he then objected to a new order from the physicians that two pages should always be in the room with him. 'He battled this long and strenuously', but in the end he gave in – for what else could he do? He could only continue to beg, without avail, that his family might come to him, or that he might be allowed to visit the Queen.

The separation from his family made him bitterly unhappy. 'I am eight and twenty years married,' he said, 'and now have no wife at all. Is not that very hard?' He begged that at the very least his children should be asked to show themselves in the garden so that he could look at them through the window, but even this was refused. One morning he got up at seven o'clock, as he had been told that the Princesses would be walking in the garden then. He stood by the window a long time; but they did not come. He did catch sight of his horses at exercise, however, which gave him a little pleasure.

At last he was told that he might have permission to see the Princesses through the window, but the first effect of this concession was to throw him into a state of agitation. 'I cannot bear it,' he said. 'No – let it be put off till evening.' When they did come, he ran to the window, meaning to fling it open, but it was screwed shut and would not move. He battered his hands against the glass and called out so desperately that Princess Elizabeth, hearing his strange, hoarse voice and seeing his distorted face through the window, came near to fainting.

The King now grew worse and none of the physicians, except Sir Lucas Pepys, could offer any comfort. He had begun to talk in a strange, wild way, saying that there had been a deluge, and that he had seen Hanover through Herschel's telescope. And Greville noted that every now and then he talked 'indecently', which he had never done while in possession of his reason. Normally he would have been 'revolted' at such expressions as he now used.

Now, too, there were the first signs of violence. He asked for his keys one day as he wanted to unlock a drawer. This was refused and he became so angry and agitated that Dr Warren was sent for. When he arrived, the King ordered him to leave the room, and when he failed to do so, he went up to him and gave him a push. Two of the equerries caught hold of the King, who then turned away, 'pale with anger and foaming with rage'. On another occasion, he gave one of his pages a 'smart slap on the face,' but he was so sorry afterwards that he took the page by the hand and asked his pardon 'twenty times'.

The Prince was still in entire charge, and the Queen therefore had no part in the decision made by the Prince and the physicians that the King should be removed from Windsor, his favourite residence, and taken to Kew Palace, which he disliked. In some ways it was a sensible decision; he would be more secluded, he would have a private garden to walk in, and it would, of course, be much more convenient for the doctors. When the Queen was informed, the Prince told her that there was no need for her to accompany the King to Kew. She said she must and would. The Prince continued to dissuade her, saying he was 'resolved upon it', and at last the Queen lost her temper. 'Prince of Wales,' she said, 'do it at your peril! Where the King is, I shall be.' He gave in, and she made arrangements to move to Kew with a part of her household.

The move was accomplished on 29 November 1788. 'I believe it was about ten o'clock when her Majesty departed,' wrote Fanny Burney. 'Drowned in tears, she glided along the passage and got softly into her carriage, with two weeping Princesses, and Lady Courtown, who was to be her Lady-in-Waiting during this dreadful residence. . . . There was not a dry eye in the house. The footmen, the housemaids, the porters, the sentinels – all cried even bitterly as they looked on.' The rest of the party, including the younger Princesses and Fanny Burney herself, was to follow later.

Arrangements for the removal of the King were more complicated, for it seemed certain that he would resist, and force was out of the question. Already rumours of ill-treatment had got about and Sir George Baker had had his carriage stopped by a crowd of angry people demanding news of the King. When he told them the news was bad, they had shouted, 'The more shame for you!' If there had been the slightest suggestion of force being used against the King, the whole country, it was thought, would have risen to defend him, and Sir Lucas Pepys believed that their own lives would be in danger.

It was decided that the King should be persuaded to go to Kew by telling him that the Queen had already left, and by promising him – falsely – that he should see her if he joined her there.

The plan did not go well. The first cautious mention of what was intended met with strong objections from the King, and he refused to leave his bed. Pitt was then called in to give the King the information that the Queen was gone, as it was thought that the King would believe him. Pitt began by remarking on the fineness of the day, and then suggested that the King might care to join the Queen who had just left. He got no further. The King said that if she had left, she had done so without his permission and must come straight back again to 'supplicate his pardon'. Other persuasions were then attempted; none had any effect. The King stayed in bed, and the Prime Minister, baffled, left him.

The Prince of Wales then told General Harcourt and Robert Greville to see what they could do. They were to tell the King that his carriage was ready and waiting, and the time now past one o'clock. The King received them civilly, made them sit by his bed and proceeded to converse with them on a variety of subjects. They urged him to get up and prepare to go to Kew, but at this he became angry, and 'hastily closed the bed curtains', shutting himself inside.

After a pause, the King tried to win them over. He knew, he said, that they were his friends and would wish to protect their King. They tried to reason with him, but the physicians, losing patience with these protracted negotiations, sent in a letter from Pitt urging the King to do what his physicians thought best for him. Once more, the King slammed shut his bed curtains, and hid himself away inside.

The physicians now gathered their courage and entered their patient's room in a body, determined to 'bring the question to a point'. The King, seeing Dr Warren among them, told him to get out of his room, and when he did not move, he jumped out of bed and ran at him. He was restrained with some difficulty and he returned to his bed. The physicians then begged the King to get ready for the move to Kew. He said he had no intention of going there. They told him he *must* go, and if he did not consent, 'other means' would be used. No,' said the King; and then, as the implications of what they had said became clear to him, he asked them bluntly whether they intended to use force. 'Yes,' he was told; if necessary, force would be used.

There was a moment's complete silence.

It is almost impossible now to imagine the impact, and the horror, of this moment for George III. A threat of force is bound to be shocking for anybody at any time, but in these circumstances – used on a man who was sick and confused, and in effect a prisoner, denied all contact with his family and with nobody at hand whom he could trust to take his side – the effect must have been terrifying beyond imagination.

Moreover, in the King's case, such a threat – uttered by men whom in normal circumstances he could have dismissed at will, men who would never ordinarily have been permitted to sit down in his presence, or even to address him unless he addressed them first – to the King such a threat must have seemed almost incredible in its sheer outrage.

Whatever George III's limitations, he was a man of immense courage, and now, ill as he was, he was able, after only a few moments' reflection, to accept and digest the fact that he was, for the time being, without power, but that he might, perhaps, manage to make conditions. He asked that General Harcourt and Robert Greville might accompany him. This was agreed, and Colonel Goldsworthy was added to the party as well.

The King now said he would get up and dress if the doctors went away; but still he lingered and invented reasons for delay, until he was reminded that he had given his word and must abide by it. He then made a start on dressing, but soon stopped and once more lay down on his bed. Colonel Manners now came in and holding up his watch in front of the King, he told him that unless he finished dressing soon, the doctors would be back to know the cause of the delay. The King, ill, threatened, and with no recourse but his own courage and what remained of his normal good sense, at last got up and dressed himself. He ate some bread and butter, drank a glass of water and went down to his carriage. He kept his nerve to the extent of saying a few words with apparent good humour to one of his gentlemen, and then, with his foot on the carriage step, he paused to ask which of his horses were in the shafts. After that, he climbed in, 'very quietly', and at last they set off for Kew. It was by now nearly a quarter to four.

As they drove through the Home Park on the way to Datchet Bridge, they saw some 'loyal inhabitants of Windsor' who had gathered to watch the King go by, and they bowed respectfully to him. He bowed back 'most kindly', and for almost the first time he allowed emotion to get the better of him. Tears came to his eyes, and hiding his face with his hands, he said, 'These good people are too fond of me'. Then he added, 'Why am I taken from a place I like best in the world?'

Again, however, he collected his courage and began to talk of other things; but the strain had been too great for him and as the journey proceeded, he began to lose control and talk and laugh and talk and talk. . . . 'His manner marked too plainly his derangement,' commented Greville. Yet he still knew what he was about, for as the carriage approached Kew, he began to allot duties to his attendants, with the clear idea of getting rid of them as soon as they arrived so that he could make a dash for the Queen.

Meanwhile, the Queen and her attendants had already arrived at Kew where they found that the Prince had put chalk marks on all the doors to indicate which room each of the party was to have. Most were discontented with the arrangements, but were prepared to put up with temporary discomfort for the King's sake, who, it was expected, would soon arrive.

But he did not. At last dinner was served; but still the King did not come. While the household was at dinner, however, there was the sound of a distant carriage approaching, and Fanny Burney jumped up and ran to the window. It was dark outside and at first she could see nothing; but the carriage came nearer and stopped, and now she could plainly hear the hoarse voice of the King talking, talking.

He jumped out of the carriage without hesitation, walked through the passage and hall in a leisurely way – and then made a sudden run. A locked door barred his way, and he was led back to the apartments which had been made ready for him. It was now that he realized – as he had clearly suspected – that the promise given him that he should see the Queen was not to be kept. 'I could not sleep all night,' wrote Fanny Burney. 'I thought I heard the poor King – his indignant disappointment haunted me.'

He accused General Harcourt and Colonel Greville of having

deceived him, although in fact they had been careful to say nothing that was not strictly true. As the evening advanced, the King became very agitated. He would *not* go to bed, he said. He would sit up and tire out his attendants. He said he was 'very strong and active', and in proof of this he 'danced and hopped with more agility', said Greville, 'than I could have suspected had been in him, but the sight of such an exhibition in our dear King and so much unlike himself, affected me most painfully.'

The next night was very bad indeed. The King became violent and 'pulled one of his pages by the hair and attempted to kick another'. He refused his meals and refused his medicines, throwing them away whenever he could. He had reached the end of endurance. He was a sick man, and he had been abused and threatened, separated from his family and forced, like any prisoner, to go where he would not. It was not a treatment to reassure him or give him confidence. 'It must be stated,' said Greville, 'that since his Majesty has been at Kew, the unfavourable symptoms of his disorder have increased.'

By 1 December, when the King had been at Kew only two days, a new and unwelcome development had to be faced by the Queen. At a Council held on 30 November it had been agreed that additional advice – advice, wrote Fanny Burney, 'such as suited only disorders that physicians in general relinquish' – must be obtained. The Queen was overwhelmed with repugnance at the idea of such a thing, for the whole world, she thought, would now know that the King's reason was affected; but she 'most painfully concurred'. She could do nothing else – she was in no position to make effective opposition.

The doctor chosen, almost certainly on the recommendation of Lady Harcourt, whose mother had been successfully treated by him, was a Dr Francis Willis. He had been a clergyman before he became a doctor and now ran a private asylum in his native county of Lincolnshire. This asylum had a good reputation and the appointment of Dr Willis was backed by William Pitt, who brought him into the King's presence himself, according to an account given by Mrs Papendiek.

7a. Filial piety, a Rowlandson cartoon of 1788 showing the Prince of Wales in his cups with his friends Colonel Hanger and Sheridan breaking into the King's bedroom interrupting the bishop praying for his recovery.

7b. The Prince of Wales by Sir Thomas Lawrence.

8. Queen Charlotte by Stroehling.

'We have found a gentleman,' he said, 'who has made the illness under which your Majesty is labouring his study for some years and we doubt not that he can render comfort, and alleviate many of the inconveniences your Majesty suffers.'

The King responded on a practical note. 'Will he let me shave myself, cut my naïls, and have a knife at breakfast and dinner?'

'Sire,' said Dr Willis, 'I am a plain man, not used to Courts, but I honour and respect my King. I know my duty and have always endeavoured to do it strictly.'

This answer appeared to satisfy the King.

VII

'I Shall Never More Wear The Crown'

The King, then, was 'mad'. Madness, however, is not strictly a medical term – it is more a description of behaviour – and from that point of view, there can be no doubt that the King was indeed mad. He was violent, he had strange ideas, he was incoherent and uncontrolled, and he behaved altogether in a way quite unlike his usual self. He took to using foul language, he had unbalanced erotic fancies, and it was even said that he had sexually assaulted a housemaid – behaviour as alien to him as could be. At times, he was deeply depressed and 'actually entreated his pages to dispatch him'. At others he became childish; he burnt some wigs belonging to his pages in a spirit of fun, he begged them to 'romp' with him, and made them wheel him about the room. At nights, he was at his worst and sometimes had to be tied to his bed.

His symptoms were recorded in great detail by his doctors, and these records have provided evidence on which various retrospective diagnoses have been made. Until recently, it was thought that he is most likely to have suffered from a manic-depressive illness, but in 1968, Dr Ida Macalpine and Dr Richard Hunter, after studying the evidence afresh, published a paper in which they tried to show that he suffered from an hereditary disorder of the metabolism known as 'porphyria'. The 'course of the royal malady reads like a description of a textbook case', they wrote. 'He had all the characteristic symptoms.' These were constipation, a painful weakness of the arms and legs, hoarseness and difficulty in swallowing, disturbances of sight and a very fast pulse. His insomnia, his state of excitement, his 'raging delirium' are all, apparently, typical of this illness and one of the royal physicians even recorded, in the King's later illness of 1811, that his urine was of a 'deeper colour, and leaves a pale blue ring upon the glass near the upper surface'. Doctors Macalpine and Hunter thought this a decisive piece of evidence, for it is from the purplish discolouration of the urine that the disease has been given the name 'porphyria'.

It is, of course, difficult to be precise in diagnosing an illness without ever seeing the patient and relying on the reports of physicians with quite different ideas from those of today, but Doctors Macalpine and Hunter seemed to have made out an overwhelmingly strong case for their belief that George III suffered from porphyria, and that a number of other members of his family suffered from it as well. These include James I and his eldest son Henry Frederick, Mary, Queen of Scots, Queen Anne, George III's sister Caroline Matilda, who perhaps died of it, his son George IV, and George IV's daughter Princess Charlotte, who may also have died of this disease.

Their conclusions, however, seem not to have been universally accepted, and informed opinion remains divided on this medical issue.

But does it matter? The question is, of course, of some historical and medical interest, but it is puzzling to see why any descendant of George III should feel pleased that the 'hereditary taint of madness' had been removed from the family by the diagnosis of porphyria. It seems a poor exchange. In severe cases of porphyria, mental derangement – that is, 'madness' – may appear and be just as pronounced as in a manic-depressive illness, while the physical symptoms are very much worse. The patient may become paralysed, delirious and suffer 'agonizing pain'. Not only that, but in the most severe attacks, the patient's life may be at risk. Porphyria is a killing disease, where 'madness' (apart from suicide), is not.

The earlier division between mental and physical illness – one being somehow a disgrace, the other sheer misfortune – has little part in medical thinking today, when the major mental illnesses are widely, though not exclusively, believed to arise from structural or metabolic changes the effects of which can often be controlled by physical methods of treatment. The one feature which divides the so-called mental illnesses from other kinds of illness is the fact that the sufferer becomes changed, or even unrecognizable, in his behaviour. He loses contact with reality, and communication with him may become almost impossible. He is cut off from everyday life, and in particular his relations with, and his feelings for, members of his family and people close to him may be totally changed; but the same is true also of porphyria, if the attack is sufficiently severe to produce mental symptoms as pronounced as those of George III.

During the early days of December, the King continued to be physically and mentally disturbed, though just occasionally his old self would show through, and he would amuse himself by drawing plans of the house and sketching out alterations. This had always been a favourite pastime. He did it methodically and 'upon a rule', and one day, after drawing a line 'pretty firmly and strait', he remarked, with one of his disconcerting flashes of insight, 'Pretty well for a man who is mad'.

The Queen and her household suffered with the King at the removal to Kew, for it had never been intended as a winter residence and it was both cold and damp. There were no floor coverings in the bedrooms and the kindly Colonel Digby went off to buy carpets for the Princesses. He could not, he told Fanny Burney, look at their rooms without shuddering and he longed to cover 'all the naked, cold boards'. In addition, he intended to purchase sandbags to try to keep out the draughts. Fanny Burney herself was given a 'pretty little new carpet' by the Queen – 'only a bedside slip but very warm'. Even the King's apartments were meagre and uncomfortable – the rooms small, the chimneys liable to smoke, and damp running down the walls.

Opinions about Dr Willis and his two sons – John, a doctor, and Thomas, a clergyman – differed from the start. They impressed

Colonel Digby as 'fine, lively, natural, independent characters', while Fanny Burney, when she eventually met them, was quite ecstatic. She thought Dr Willis a 'man in ten thousand, open, honest, dauntless and high-minded', and his son John very nearly his equal. Others, however, thought Dr Willis 'not much better than a mountebank', and there was certainly an element of brutality in his treatment of his patients. He was accustomed to break them in, he said, like horses. This was not out of line with the sort of treatment which most sufferers from mental illnesses received at that period, and it was probably sincerely intended for the good of the patient. It was at a later date, when Dr Willis himself was no longer in charge, that the Willis family took on a positively sinister character and even went so far, on one occasion, as to make a serious attempt to kidnap the King – for his own good, naturally.

On 5 December Dr Willis had his first formal interview with the King and found him composed and apparently determined to impress on him that although he had been extremely ill, he was now quite well again. He complained bitterly of his doctors, and then went on to remark that Dr Willis, judging by his dress and appearance, belonged to the Church. Dr Willis said that this had been true in the past, but that he had now turned to the practice of medicine.

'I am sorry for it,' said the King. 'You have quitted a profession I have always loved, and you have embraced one I most heartily detest.'

Dr Willis replied that 'Our Saviour' went about healing the sick.

'Yes,' answered the King crisply, 'but he had not £700 a year for it.'

The King then suggested to Dr Willis that Dr Warren would make an ideal inmate for his asylum in Lincolnshire.

Although the King took the arrival of Dr Willis with apparent calm, he was perfectly aware of the implications and felt them deeply. He told one of his pages that he could 'never more show his face again in this country, that he would leave it for ever and retire to Hanover'.

[101]

That evening Dr Willis and the King had another interview, and once again the King launched into abuse of doctors and medicine. Dr Willis told him that he stood in urgent need of medical treatment for 'his ideas were now deranged'. He hoped, however, to be of use to the King. The King, now 'violently enraged', rushed at Dr Willis, but he stood his ground and said that the King must control himself, as otherwise he would be put in a strait waistcoat.

He then left the room and returned carrying one under his arm. The King 'eyed it attentively' and then began to 'submit'. He agreed to go to bed; but after Dr Willis had left the room, he broke down. Why had his other doctors dealt so unfairly with him, he asked, and concealed from him his real situation? 'After this,' writes Greville, 'the poor dear King, overcome by his feelings, burst into a flood of tears and wept bitterly.'

It was certainly shock treatment of a sort, but the kindly and scrupulous Colonel Greville, judging by the standards of his day, was favourably impressed. He was greatly struck by the 'authoritative language' of Dr Willis, and thought this struggle and its outcome absolutely necessary and the 'first solid step leading to permanent recovery' which had yet taken place. There was indeed one good result. Dr Willis, who now displaced the other physicians and held the chief authority in the management of the King, took a steadily optimistic view about the possibility of complete recovery, and he was largely responsible for staving off the passing of a Regency Bill. 'A little more time I ask for,' he used to say. 'Even as days go on, I do not despair.'

William Pitt depended on the King for his own survival as Prime Minister and for the survival of his government. Since the opposing party – the Whigs – was led by Charles James Fox, a friend of the Prince of Wales, there seemed no doubt that if the Prince became Regent, Fox would lead a new government. Already Fox and his followers had been having a happy time dealing round the leading offices of state, and their jubilation soon reached indecent proportions. Card players at Brooks's Club said, 'I play the lunatic', when they put down a King, and the Prince, drinking and celebrating with his friends, exercised his remarkable gift for mimicry by imitating his father's ravings. In his excitement at the brilliant prospects opening before him, he seemed to have lost all natural concern for his father.

On 3 December a Privy Council had been held at which the doctors had been commanded to attend and give their opinions as to whether the King was in a state to transact business. All agreed that this was, at present, out of the question. On the possibility of his ultimate recovery, all except Dr Warren – the Prince's doctor and firm supporter – were guarded but not hopeless. The Prince, however, in writing to his brother Augustus, had none of the inhibitions of the doctors and told him that their father's state had now 'grown to such a pitch that he is a compleat lunatick'. From this time onwards the doctors were constantly summoned to give their accounts of the King and this, on top of the care of his patient, came near to being too much for the elderly Dr Willis. Nothing but pity and loyalty, he said, kept him at his post, worn out as he was by insults and endless waiting on Parliamentary committees. He remained, however, steadfast in his conviction that the King would recover, whatever the present setbacks.

These were many. During this period the strait waistcoat was put on the King for the first time, and on the following day he kept repeating over and over again that he would 'never more wear the crown'. He had also been lashed to the bed, and there were 'great wars and rumours of wars', so it was said, 'among the medical tribe'.

'Great wars' also between the rival factions in parliament. Charles James Fox overplayed his hand at the start by claiming that the Prince had a 'natural right' not only to be Regent, but to be given the full powers of a Regent without delay. Pitt could not deny, of course, that if a Regency became necessary, the Prince had the first and indisputable claim, but he felt that some restrictions were called for, and he introduced a Regency Bill which left the royal household and the care of the King's person in the hands of the Queen, and denied the Prince the right to create peerages except on behalf of his brothers. The rights of the King, if he should recover, were also safeguarded.

The Opposition were outraged, though couching all their objections in moving terms based on the natural affection between father and son, and repugnance at the idea of entrusting the care of the King's person to one 'not of his Majesty's blood' – in other words, his wife. In fact, they found it unbearable that the Prince would not be able to distribute peerages among his friends and supporters, and that the rich posts of the royal household were to be denied them.

'Is it the House of Hanover or the House of Strelitz that is to govern the country?' they asked. The Queen might be drawn aside from the paths of rectitude, but all knew the sterling integrity of the Prince's character. The trouble was that his character was but too well known, and the idea of putting him in charge of the royal household seemed less than attractive.

The doctors were now become, in effect, the 'men in power', as Burke put it, for the fortunes of the Regency Bill rested largely on what they could be induced to say. Dr Warren became ever more pessimistic, while Dr Willis continued to have 'great hopes'. Pitt pointed out in Parliament that Dr Willis had the greater experience in the 'particular disorder' with which his Majesty was afflicted, while Dr Warren, though in other ways no doubt an excellent physician, had little or none. 'Were they going to rob the first physician in this country of his character?' called out Burke, while Sheridan mildly deplored any attempt to decide between the merits of rival physicians; all the same, he added, he did find Dr Willis a trifle 'prevaricating and evasive' in his answers.

Meanwhile, at Kew, the King seemed momentarily a little better and on 11 December he had his first walk in the gardens; but the next day brought a setback. The strait waistcoat was brought out again, his legs were tied up and he was 'secured down across his breast'. The King, in fact, was feeling the impact of Dr Willis's belief in firm control. But with the remnants of practical good sense which kept asserting themselves even at the darkest moments of his illness, he made efforts to cooperate. A few days later, when he had once again been bound down, he begged to be released. Dr Willis asked him if he could trust to his honour to be quiet if he did release him, and the King replied that he would do his best – 'which was all a man could do'.

Although at times he was quieter, in some ways his mind seemed more seriously deranged than before. He became very angry on Christmas Day because he had wanted the Archbishop of Canterbury to come and administer the Sacrament. Crawling under the sofa, he said that as 'everything had been denied him, he would there converse with his Saviour and no one could interrupt them'. Papendiek, one of the pages, got under the sofa with him and then gave orders for it to be lifted up so that the King could be put on his bed. Once there, he proceeded to hug his pillow, declaring it was Prince Octavius, who had, he declared, been 'new-born this day'.

It was soon after this that he developed the fancy, which persisted until his recovery and reappeared in his later illnesses, that he was in love with Lady Pembroke, a woman whom he had known all his life and who was by now a respectable grandmother of over fifty. She had even walked in his wedding procession, looking, according to Horace Walpole, 'a picture of majestic modesty'. The King now began to assert that she was his Queen and Charlotte an imposter. But even then, he could often show some awareness of his mental state, for he told one of his pages that he hoped nobody knew what 'wrong things' he had said about her.

It is impossible to guess how much of the King's turbulence and violent behaviour was purely due to his illness, and how much to a sense of outrage at his situation, for in addition to physical restraints, Dr Willis presumed to lecture him on his improper fancies and on the indecency of his language. When the King attempted to protest, a handkerchief was forcibly held in front of his mouth while Dr Willis proceeded with his lecture. The sheer impertinence of it all must have seemed breathtaking to the King. On top of this, there was the continual discomfort and pain not only of his illness, but of the remedies. The blisters applied to his legs and other parts of his body were a continual source of pain, he was prescribed musk which smelt so peculiarly horrible that he begged – unavailingly – not to be forced to take it, and even when he wanted to go to sleep, he often had to endure the misery of being tied down. 'How,' he asked, 'could a man sleep with his legs tied to the bed-posts?'

It is a remarkable proof of his physical stamina and his courage that, in the end, he did make progress. Even the strait waistcoat he learned to accept with philosophy, good-humouredly wearing it unfastened under his coat so that it could be tied up the more easily when necessary. 'Heavens,' exclaimed Greville, 'what a spectacle to see the dear afflicted King standing in a strait waistcoat and tucking up himself the sleeves and strings until they might be wanted!' And when a special chair – a 'chair of correction' – was brought into the room, the King was even able to achieve a wry joke by calling it his 'Coronation Chair' and arranging it in some state at the head of the room.

The physicians continued to quarrel, and the Regency Bill continued on its slow way, but by the end of the year 1788 it had still not become law. Dr Willis was now maintaining that he saw unmistakeable signs of improvement in the King, but Dr Warren still argued that although the King might speak '6 or 7 or more rational sentences than usual . . . he would not allow him better, for if he was insane, he was insane'. He did not consider that there were degrees in disorders of this type.

Outside, the fight to achieve power for the Prince was splitting fashionable London into two violently opposed camps. The ladies of the Opposition wore large caps 'à la Régence' – confections with the motto 'Ich dien' nestling in a mountainous froth of gauze with three long feathers in front; a 'collection of trumpery', said Lord Harcourt, and costing a ridiculous sum. Mrs Thrale was no less disgusted at these goings-on. 'The Opposition catch greedily at the notion of his being a confined lunatick,' she wrote. 'Poor man! How distressful is his situation!'

'Distressful' indeed it was, for on top of all his other miseries, it was now decided that he should be largely deprived of the society of his equerries, whom he knew well, and left in the hands of his pages, with whom he was naturally on terms of far less intimacy. And still he longed, above all things, for his wife and children. He would often look at a picture of the Queen and say, 'We have been married twenty-eight years, and never have been separated a day till now, and now you abandon me in my misfortunes.' On this one matter, Dr Willis, so severe in his methods of restraint, showed a kindlier and more imaginative attitude than the other doctors, and on 28 December he went upstairs to suggest to the Queen that she should visit the King. Even so the visit was limited to a quarter of an hour and Dr Willis stayed in the room the whole time. 'We could hear the King's voice,' wrote Greville, 'but without hearing his conversation – and at times he appeared to us to be crying.'

The King had, apparently, received the Queen very kindly, often kissing her hand. Dr Willis could not follow their conversation as it had been conducted in German, but if the King's later account was correct, it was not entirely kind, for he claimed that he had told the Queen that he did not like her and preferred another, that she was mad and had been so for the last three years, and that he would on no account admit her to his bed until 1793 – 'for reasons,' said Greville, 'he then improperly explained'. After the Queen had gone, the King became very agitated indeed, abusing Dr Willis and calling him an old fool.

By the beginning of January, improvement seemed more definite and on New Year's Day, Dr Willis gave Pitt 'the most flattering accounts' of the King's progress, making the hardly flattering claim that he was now as capable of transacting business of State as 'ever he had been in his life'. It was more a proof of Dr Willis's partisanship than anything else, for that evening the King was once more out of control and singing ditties about his imagined love, Lady Pembroke – in particular a song of which the first verse ran:

> I made love to Kate,
> Long I sighed for she,
> Till I heard of late
> That she'd a mind of me!

Subsequent verses were distinctly bawdy.

On 6 January 1789 it was decided that the physicians must be once more examined about the prospects of the King's recovery, as his inability to deal with public business was becoming serious; but as usual the physicians could not agree. Sir Lucas Pepys was cautiously optimistic, Dr Willis completely confident, while Warren and Baker, supported by one of the other physicians, professed themselves unable to see any improvement in the King's condition at all.

The Opposition now pressed for an immediate and unrestricted Regency. The disorder with which the Sovereign was afflicted, declared Burke, was like a 'vast sea which rolled in and at a low tide rolled back and left a bald and barren shore'. He had taken pains to inform himself on the subject of insanity, he had 'turned over every book upon it', and had visited the 'dreadful mansions' where such sufferers were confined. He had also read enough to feel a 'sense of the danger of an uncertain cure' and the possibilities of relapse. Dr Willis, unperturbed, told Lady Harcourt that while the politicians were disputing, the King was recovering and they would 'kick all their castles into the dust'. Dr Warren, for his part, bustled about purveying titbits of information to his patients and giving an 'improperly particular account' of the various changes in the King's health.

Dr Willis now took to prescribing emetics which were secretly introduced into the King's food, with such effect that the King knelt on a chair and prayed that 'God would be pleased either to restore him to his senses or permit that he might die directly'. It looked as though his prayer would be answered, for there were now longer intervals when he was able to be comparatively rational. He played games of backgammon with Dr Willis and conversed in Latin with Sir Lucas Pepys, for he had been taking the opportunity, as he said later, to 'brush up his Latin' – an impressive effort for a man in his state of health who had never shown any bent for scholarship. But there were, of course, setbacks. On one occasion, when he had been given permission to go 'for an airing', he filled his pockets with a strange jumble of objects

– two or three pairs of stockings, a couple of nightcaps, a pair of drawers, a pack of cards and some counters – evidently with the intention of making a dash for Lady Pembroke, his 'Queen Elizabeth', as he called her. He also made a practice of carrying the Queen of Hearts about in his pocket, often kissing it and calling it Lady Pembroke's portrait.

It is not known how much of all this reached the Queen's ears, but, not surprisingly, she 'drooped'. Her hair had gone quite grey during these months and she was 'worn to a skeleton' – so much so that her corsets, it was said, would go round her twice.

On 2 February, the King had his famous encounter with Fanny Burney in Kew Gardens. Like everybody else, she had been warned always to keep out of the King's way, but on this occasion she had been told – wrongly – that the King would not be in the gardens. He was. He caught sight of her and hailed her with enthusiasm, obviously delighted to see a familiar face. She, very much frightened, took to her heels. So did he. She ran faster still; and so did he, calling and hallooing after her in his strange hoarse voice. Ever faster they went, the King after Miss Burney, the doctors after the King, the attendants after the doctors, all calling as they went. At last she realized they were telling her to stop as so much running might harm the King. Reluctantly, she slowed her pace, and the King came panting up and kissed her roundly on the cheek. She was very taken aback by this salute, but his good humour was unmistakeable. He poured out anything and everything that came into his head as they walked up and down, from descriptions of changes he proposed to make in his establishment to assurances that she need no longer be bullied by Mrs Schwellenberg.

'Never mind her!' he said. 'Don't be oppressed! I am your friend. Don't let her cast you down! I know you have a hard time of it, but don't mind her!' He stopped walking for emphasis. 'I will protect you! I promise you that – and therefore depend upon me!'

The doctors tried to put an end to the conversation.

'No, no, no, no!' cried the King, continuing to walk. He then embarked on a history of his pages and how disgracefully they had behaved to him. These complaints seem to have had some basis in fact, particularly in the case of 'Mr Ernst'.

He then burst into song and 'ran over' most of Handel's Oratorios, attempting several airs and choruses, but he was so 'dreadfully hoarse' that the sound was far from euphonious.

Dr Willis now became positively alarmed and again tried to separate them, but the King had not nearly finished his conversation. He spoke of Mrs Delany – 'She was my friend!' he cried, wiping his eyes, 'and I loved her as a friend.'

Dr Willis again intervened, but, 'No, no!' said the King. 'I want to ask Miss Burney a few questions. I have lived so long out of the world, I know nothing.'

On they walked and the King made enquiries about his friends, spoke very kindly about her father and then assured her that when he could get away from his doctors, he would 'rule with a rod of iron'.

Now at last he was induced – reluctantly – to let her go, and she hurried off to the Queen with the news that she had talked with the King and that he had been very nearly his usual self. On the following evening, the Queen herself visited him, this time accompanied by Princess Augusta and Princess Elizabeth. He was again in good spirits – perhaps rather *too* good, for he proposed a little singing and the party could be plainly heard belting out 'Rule Britannia' and 'Come Cheer up my Lads'. 'Where so much gloom has been,' commented Greville, 'the hilarity of the present moment should be welcome, tho' in truth it partook more of the jollity of an election than the etiquette of a Court.' He was relieved, however, a few days later when the King refrained from greeting his family with a serenade on his flute, an instrument he had been practising during his illness. His familiar 'What – what – what!' had also begun to be heard again, and this was taken to be an encouraging sign, for it had disappeared from his speech during the whole of the time he had been ill.

On 12 February a 'progressive state of amendment' was formally announced and Sir George Baker was obliged to admit that the

King had talked rationally for twenty-five minutes. Even Dr Warren found him 'considerably better'. His pulse was slowing down to a more normal rate and the other physical symptoms were subsiding. A 'state of convalescence' was announced on 17 February; on the 19th the Regency Bill was dropped in the Lords and in the Commons on the following day.

The King, however, had no illusions about the difficulties he must still face. 'Believe me,' he said to Greville, 'I have no child's play before me, but all will do well by degrees.' He was still not entirely in control of his speech and the Queen confided to Lady Harcourt that when he felt he was about to say something wrong, he 'put his hand upon his mouth and said "Hush" '. And there was one thing in particular that worried him – what exactly had, or had not, happened between himself and Lady Pembroke? At last he nerved himself to ask her outright, and she reassured him at once. Her feelings for him had always been, and still were, those of a 'most affectionate sister towards an indulgent brother'.

The Prince and the Duke of York now made formal application to see their father, the King, but he did not feel able to face the meeting immediately and the interview was fixed for 23 February. They arrived, with incredible rudeness, two and a half hours late, but the King still received them. He kept the conversation to safe topics such as his new interest in improving his Latin, and he told them he had learned to play picquet. His composure and natural-ness of manner meant the final death of all their bright hopes of power, and they went off afterwards to try to drown their dis-appointment in 'wine and dissipation'. They even tried to pretend that their father was not better at all, but as mad as ever, at last provoking Chancellor Thurlow to remark, 'By God! I suppose they wind up the King whenever I go to Kew, for he seems always well when I see him.' They had gone too far and disgusted everybody. 'I believe,' wrote Lord Bulkeley, 'that the King's mind is torn to pieces by his sons.'

The King now felt able to see Pitt, who found his manner 'un-usually composed and dignified', and on 26 February a final bulletin was issued pronouncing 'an entire cessation of his Majesty's illness'.

Early in March, he found he could once more listen to music with pleasure and the evening concerts were resumed; and now once more he shared the Queen's bedroom.

His return to health was celebrated everywhere and the Queen had a private celebration of her own at Kew Palace at which 'Providence, Health and Britannia' were displayed with 'elegant devices'. The King watched from a window while the Queen, covered in jewels almost from head to foot, sat in state receiving her guests, and making it very plain from her manner what she had thought of their behaviour during the King's illness. She was immensely happy and was soon writing to her friend, Lady Harcourt, in terms of unaccustomed frivolity, telling her that she proposed eating chicken 'in order to appear more beautiful when I see you next; but in case it does not succeed, believe me equally, handsome as chicken can make me or ugly as I am, your sincere friend, Charlotte'.

A Thanksgiving service for the King's recovery was held in St Paul's Cathedral on 23 April, but the Archbishop of Canterbury tried to persuade him not to go to it in case it might be too much of a strain; but he was determined to be there. 'My lord,' he said, 'I have twice read over the evidence of the physicians on my case, and if I can stand that, I can stand anything.' It was a long service lasting several hours, but the King remained dignified and composed throughout, in strong contrast to the Princes, who chatted, waved to friends and even, so it was said, munched biscuits during the sermon.

In June the King set off for a holiday at Weymouth, which was such a success that Weymouth became a favourite place for royal holidays ever afterwards. Cheering crowds greeted him all the way on the journey down, and at Weymouth itself the enthusiasm was almost embarrassing. 'God save the King' was emblazoned on shop-fronts, caps, and bathing-machines, and even the bathing-women wore it 'in large letters round their waists to encounter the waves'. When the King went bathing, a band of fiddlers, hidden in a nearby bathing-machine, struck up 'God Save the King' the minute the royal head went under the water.

They returned to Windsor in September with the King's illness now behind him. He was well and in good spirits, and he settled down to attend to business and live his life as usual; but he was not quite the same. Now, for the first time, he began to consider his health. He no longer rode his horses – or his equerries – quite so hard, and on bad days, said the Queen, 'when the clouds threaten us with storms', he would 'readily stay at home', a thing he had never done before. And he told William Pitt that although he did not want any measures 'unnecessarily delayed', he must decline 'entering upon a pressure of business'. 'Indeed, for the rest of my life,' he said, 'I shall expect others to fulfil the duties of their employment and only keep that superintending eye which can be effected without labour and fatigue.'

It was a change indeed from his early days as King.

VIII

Alarms and Entanglements

The King was now well, and he was thankful to see the last of the Willises of whom he had no affectionate memories. He gave them suitable presents, however, and pensions were agreed for them after a certain amount of acrimony and bickering, accompanied on their part by protests that they had been promised more. But they did quite well in the end for, as a direct result of the *réclame* they had won through George III's recovery, they were called in to treat the Queen of Portugal, similarly afflicted, on highly profitable terms.

The King was naturally anxious to get rid of the pages who had seen him in such disarray, since it would clearly be difficult to secure from them a proper degree of respect; but here he ran into unexpected difficulties. 'Mr Ernst', in particular, who had been rude and obstructive while attending the King during his illness and had even been known to sit down in his presence with his hat on, was very disinclined to be dismissed unless he was well compensated. He was offered a full salary on retirement and apartments in St James's. But what about all my perquisites? he asked. They could not be granted, he was told. 'But surely after such long and faithful service. . . .' 'No,' he was told. Then he would refuse to be dismissed, he said, unless a sum equivalent to his accustomed perquisites in food, candles and so on was added to his salary. This was refused. Ernst was full of indignation – were all his months of arduous and anxious labour to receive no recognition? It seemed that they were. In the end, after a disagreeable wrangle, the dismissals had to be withdrawn and a rearrangement of duties worked out instead. Only one page – Stillingfleet – was willing to leave.

The King found himself able to resume public life with less embarrassment than he had foreseen, to some extent confirming Mrs Thrale's bracing edict that a 'madman is *never* ashamed of being mad. I remember,' she said, 'Lord Mulgrave saying many years ago that it sharpened the wits and made men more agreeable for their whole lives to come.'

Whether the King was more agreeable or not, the Queen was decidedly less so, for from about this time onwards there were increasing comments about her peevishness and bad temper. She had had enough. She had spent over twenty years in almost uninterrupted childbearing, she had endured the terrors and anxieties of seeing her husband apparently insane, and in a state which frightened her exceedingly. She wished to make no more efforts for anybody – except to continue, in a quiet way, to give to the charities which she conscientiously, and perhaps a little coldly, supported. She was a cold woman in many ways, and had particularly little sympathy for illness. Even Fanny Burney, who wrote, as a rule, in such saccharine terms of the 'sweet Queen', had to admit that illness in court circles was 'commonly supposed' to be 'wilful' and therefore met with little kindness or attention. When she herself was very ill indeed, and was forced to ask permission to leave, she found that she was treated with noticeably diminished cordiality by the Queen, who seemed to be of the opinion that she ought rather to have struggled on, live or die, than resign.

The King was kinder. When the apothecary of Windsor, for instance, who had been attending him during his illness, fell and injured himself, the King made a point of going to sit with him. saying, 'You took care of my illness. It's my turn to nurse you now.' And when his son, Frederick, Duke of York, had a narrow escape in a duel with Colonel Lennox, he ran and took him in his arms the next time they met, and burst into tears. The Queen acted very differently. Although the Prince of Wales had particularly asked her not to receive Colonel Lennox, she treated him with good humour when next he presented himself at court, while she turned coldly away from Frederick, remarking that the whole affair was far more likely to have been his fault than anybody else's.

It may have taken courage on the King's part to enter into public and social life again, given all the indignities of his illness and the rumours spread abroad about his ravings and violence, but when he did make the effort, he found that his illness had enormously increased his popularity. People in general were sorry for him and for all that he had suffered, and they had been shocked beyond expression by the brutal behaviour of his two eldest sons. 'I could tell you,' wrote Lady Harcourt, 'some particulars of the Prince of Wales's behaviour towards the King and Queen . . . that would make your blood run cold.' Many people did not need to be told, for they had seen at first hand the heartless enthusiasm with which they had greeted any deterioration in the King's condition, the gusto with which they had spread stories of his ravings and their reluctance to believe him better. Soon after the King's recovery, the Prince was surrounded by a hostile mob as he drove to the Opera, and he was frequently jeered at in the streets; but the King was cheered.

Gradually George III grew more relaxed and resumed his friendly habit of dropping in on his neighbours. It was a habit that was not altogether appreciated, for the sudden arrival of royalty was enough to throw any household into confusion. Even in these circumstances, the strict demands of etiquette could not be wholly put on one side and frantic preparations had to be made, sometimes at a few minutes warning. Horace Walpole complained of having to jump up from a sick-bed and being obliged to stand for long hours on end at a surprise visit from royalty. The King's unheralded calls on humbler households probably caused less consternation for at least the labouring classes were not expected to provide suitable refreshment and observe protocol, and they probably got some sort of a present in money or goods.

A number of attempts on the King's life were made during the ten or twelve years after his illness, but he met them with his usual unflinching courage. An attempt was made to kill him with an airgun in 1794 when he was out driving. The bolt passed right through the carriage just near where he was sitting, and Lord Chesterfield, who was with him, instinctively ducked to avoid being hit.

'What – do you *duck* my lord?' exclaimed the King.

'It was time, I think,' said Chesterfield. 'Why, it only very nearly missed us.'

'Well, well,' said the King. 'If we are to die, let us die like gentlemen – and not *duck*!'

Another attempt was made the following year, in October 1795, this time when the King was driving in his State Coach to open Parliament, attended by the Earl of Westmoreland and Lord Onslow. 'Before I sleep,' wrote Lord Onslow that night, 'let me bless God for the miraculous escape which my King, my country and myself have had this day.'

There had been a good deal of unrest in the country for some years, chiefly as a result of the social upheaval which the In-dustrial Revolution had brought with it. In addition, the enclos-ure movement on the land and the change from small farms to large, from hand labour to a certain degree of mechanization, had meant the loss of employment in the country and a conse-quent drift into the towns. There people were crowded together in hideous conditions, often hungry, often unable to find work. Even if they did find work, they were still poor, for prices rose very rapidly while wages did not. In addition, the war against France which had broken out in 1793 was going badly. 'Vast meet-ings were held in the open air', there were bread riots, and in 1793 the King's speech to Parliament even mentioned a 'con-spiracy to destroy the Constitution and subvert law and order'. The government embarked on a series of repressive measures and in 1795 the Seditious Meetings Act forbade more than fifty persons to meet together without first notifying a magistrate. 'It was an awful time for those who had the misfortune to entertain liberal opinions,' said Sydney Smith.

It was against this background of anger and unrest that the King set out to open Parliament in 1795. As they drove through the park, they noticed that there was an unusually large crowd of people and a 'sullen silence seemed to prevail'. 'No hats – or at least very few – were pulled off,' noted Lord Onslow, 'little or no huzzaing, and frequently a cry of "Give us bread" or "No war"; and once or twice "No King", with "hissing and groaning".' Nothing serious happened, however, until they reached the narrowest part of the street called St Margaret's, between the two palace yards. They had passed the Office of Ordnance and were 'just opposite the parlour window of the house adjoining it', when a small ball, either of lead or marble, penetrated the glass window to the right of the King, making a small hole in it. It passed right through the coach and went out by the far window which happened to be open.

'This is a shot!' exclaimed Lord Onslow.

The King betrayed no sign of fear whatsoever, and when they reached the House of Lords merely remarked to the Lord Chancellor, when he came to meet him, 'My Lord, we have been shot at.' He then put on his robes and read his speech with 'peculiar correctness'.

'Well, my lords,' he said, as they got into the coach to drive home, 'one person is *proposing* this, and another is *supposing* that, forgetting that there is One above us who *disposes* of everything, and on whom alone we depend.'

As they neared St James's, they saw that the mob in the park had by now grown even larger, and that it was composed of the 'worst and lowest sort'. Insults were shouted at them and stones were thrown, several hitting the King; but he showed no sign of indignation or resentment. 'The glasses were all broken to pieces,' wrote Lord Onslow, 'and in this situation we were during our passage through the park. The King took one of the stones out of the cuff of his coat where it had lodged and gave it to me, saying, "I make you a present of this, as a mark of the civilities we have met with on our journey today!" '

In August 1800 two attempts on his life were made in one day. At a review of the Grenadier Guards in the morning, five shots were fired at him. They missed, but a young man was hit in the leg. The second attack was made on him that night in the theatre at Drury Lane. Accompanied by the Queen and some of the Princesses, he had gone to see Colley Cibber's play, *She would and She would Not*, and as he entered the royal box and went forward to bow to the audience two shots were fired at him by a man in the front row of the pit. The King instinctively stepped back, but almost at once, pulling himself together, he deliberately went forward to the front of the box, put his opera glasses to his eyes and looked round the house.

He signalled to the Queen, who was following him into the box, to keep back, calling over his shoulder to her, 'It's only a squib, a squib. They are firing squibs for diversion.' The Lord Chamberlain, the Earl of Salisbury, then begged him to retire to the safety of the ante-room.

'Sir, you discompose me as well as yourself,' the King told him. 'I shall not stir one step.'

By this time, the would-be assassin – a man called Watkins – had been seized by members of the audience and dragged into the music-room below the stage.

'We will not stir,' repeated the King, 'but see the entertainment out.'

The Queen was now allowed to join him and they sat through the play exactly as usual, the King even taking his accustomed doze of three or four minutes between the end of the play and the beginning of the farce which followed it.

'I should have despised myself for ever,' he said afterwards, 'had I but stirred a single inch. A man on such an occasion should need no prompting, but immediately see what is his duty.'

Later on, after he had arrived safely home, he said that he had no doubt that he would be able to sleep that night as well as he always did. 'My prayer is that the poor unhappy person who aimed at my life may rest as quietly as I shall.' The 'unhappy person' turned out to be a man of the 15th Dragoons who had been severely wounded in the head in battle. He was declared to be mad and sent to Bedlam.

The King was at his best giving these exhibitions of Hanoverian courage and Christian forbearance; he was *not* at his best in his treatment of his children. It is true that he received considerable provocation from his sons, but so did they from him, and much of their behaviour can be traced to the harshness, the general lack of consideration – even the lack of love – which they experienced from him once early childhood was behind them. One small incident is typical of the lack of grace he was apt to show in his dealings with his sons. The King had been recommended to drink wine in small quantities as an aid to digestion during his convalescence, and the Prince of Wales gracefully sent him a few bottles of the finest Madeira that the island – so he said – had ever produced. He proposed tasting it with the King when the family dined together. The King refused. He thanked him, but said that he hoped the best wine was *always* provided at his table. For himself, he was sure the wine would do him more harm than good.

Of course, the Prince's behaviour was a continual harassment to the King, and his debts became increasingly a public scandal. By 1792 they had reached the astronomical sum of £400,000. Something had to be done. The Lord Chancellor approached the King, who could only suggest, with some lack of realism, that 'moderate retrenchment' would be advisable; or, of course, the Prince might marry and his allowance would then automatically be increased by a considerable amount.

To force the Prince into marriage as the only way of improving a desperate financial situation seems rather disreputable; even less attractive, perhaps, is the fact that the Prince was willing to accept it as a way out of his difficulties, in spite of his long-standing relationship with Mrs Fitzherbert and in spite of the determination he had often expressed never to marry. 'I will never marry,' he had told Lord Malmesbury. 'My resolution is taken on that subject. I have settled it with Frederick. No – I never will marry! Frederick will marry and the crown will descend to his children.' His change of mind may, of course, have been influenced by the fact that none of his brothers – including Frederick – had as yet produced any legitimate children, although William was busy fathering a brood of bastards, eventually numbering ten, on the actress, Mrs Jordan. And of course mistresses, however long-established and faithful, traditionally have to give way when more regular alliances are in prospect.

At all events, a marriage for the Prince of Wales was decided upon, but the choice of an actual bride seems to have been treated with comparative indifference – almost as a detail – by both the Prince and his father. The King eventually expressed a preference for his niece Caroline of Brunswick, the daughter of his sister Augusta, and the Prince raised no objection, giving the impression that one dowdy German princess was no less dreary than any other. So the King requested Lord Malmesbury to make a formal demand for her hand on behalf of the Prince.

Malmesbury stressed afterwards that he had been given no latitude whatever – that he had not been asked to advise, and so felt unable to express any opinion about the suitability or otherwise of Caroline as a bride for the Prince. But given that he had been on fairly confidential terms with the Prince for some time, it seems a little strange that he gave no hint of a warning of what his proposed bride was really like. The Prince never forgave him.

The Queen *had* received a warning, but even more strangely she kept silence because she thought it 'unseemly' to speak to the King in a way that was unflattering to his niece. 'But it is not at all unseemly,' she wrote to her brother Charles of Mecklenburg-Strelitz, 'to tell you that a relative of that family has spoken to me of Princess Caroline with very little respect. They say that her passions are so strong that the Duke himself said that she was not to be allowed even to go from one room to another without her Governess, and that when she dances, this lady is obliged to follow her for the whole of the dance to prevent her from making an exhibition of herself by indecent conversations with men . . . and that all amusements have been forbidden her because of her indecent conduct.' Yet the Queen gave no hint of this knowledge to her own son who was proposing to marry the girl.

Malmesbury considered that Caroline's appearance was not un-satisfactory; she was a reasonably pretty girl of twenty-seven years, with fair hair, light eyebrows and rather good teeth ('but going'). Her figure was not particularly graceful, but she had a 'good bust' and 'what the French call "des épaules impertinentes" '. Her appearance could well have struck the Prince as rather better than he might have expected; it was her character which was the trouble. As the Queen had been warned, she was over-fond of men, and she may – in spite of supervision – have already had love affairs. She was certainly indiscreet in her general behaviour. 'Elle n'est pas bête,' said her father, 'mais elle n'a pas de juge-ment.'

Acting on this hint, Lord Malmesbury spent considerable time in giving her social advice, telling her not to talk so much, to re-strain her natural inquisitiveness and to maintain a dignity and reserve suitable to her future rank. She was touchingly good-tempered in the face of all this criticism and advice, but showed small sign of being able to benefit by it. She had no 'fonds', thought Lord Malmesbury, 'no fixed character, a light and flighty mind, but meaning well and well-disposed'.

Caroline was a little downcast, not unnaturally, when she heard that her mother had received a letter from her future father-in-law, the King, hoping that his niece would not have 'trop de vivacité, et qu'elle menera une vie sédentaire et retirée'. She was quite intelligent enough to see that she would never fit very well into this picture. She was positively startled, however, when Lord Malmesbury thought it necessary to warn her that marital in-fidelity on her part would be regarded as high treason.

As a potential bride for the Prince of Wales, she had even more serious drawbacks than susceptibility and a bouncing familiarity with her social inferiors. She was a slattern. Lord Malmesbury distastefully noted that she wore 'coarse petticoats, coarse shifts, and thread stockings, and these never well washed or changed often enough'. Nor was she washed often enough her-self. To put it bluntly, she smelt. She was accustomed to boast of her quickness in dressing, but Lord Malmesbury bravely tackled her on the subject of cleanliness and told her that a long *toilette* was necessary. She must pay the most careful attention to cleanliness and to everything concerning dress if she was to please the Prince. Good-natured as ever, Caroline took all this criticism in good part and appeared next day 'well washed *all over*'. A less compatible bride for the sophisticated, fastidious Prince of Wales could scarcely have been found.

In March 1795 Caroline set out on her journey to England. She had already heard rumours that the Prince had a favourite mistress – this was Lady Jersey, a grandmother and the mother of two sons and seven daughters. As the popular rhyme went:

> *Among the whole, not one in ten*
> *Could please him like a tough old hen.*

Caroline herself was inclined to giggle about it until reproved by Lord Malmesbury. She may not, however, have expected to find Lady Jersey in the party sent to welcome her at Greenwich; and not only that, but a Lady Jersey self-confident enough to make difficulties. She could not, she said, sit backwards in a coach and must be allowed to sit forward. Lord Malmesbury told her with some firmness that it was impossible and that if she found sitting backwards disagreed with her, she should never have accepted the position of one of the Princess's ladies. If she was really likely to be sick, he told her, then she must travel in another carriage. That settled the difficulty; she sat facing backwards.

At St James's, the Princes of Wales met Caroline for the first time and took a dislike to her on sight. She attempted to kneel to him and he raised her up with characteristic grace; but he then turned away abruptly and left her. 'I am not well,' he told Lord Malmesbury. 'Pray get me a glass of brandy.' Malmesbury suggested that water might be better. 'No,' said the Prince with an oath, and left the room. The Princess was amazed. 'Mon Dieu!' she said, 'does the Prince always behave like that? He seems to me horribly fat and not nearly so good-looking as his portrait.'

It was true he was fat – two years later he was said to weigh seventeen stone and eight pounds; but although his appearance may have been a shock to her, it is hard to see why he was so upset by hers. She was by no means bad-looking and Lord Malmesbury would have seen to it that on this occasion at least she was well-washed. She had had as yet no opportunity to display her hoydenish ways – indeed she had done no more than attempt to kneel to him. Perhaps he felt some intuition of what was to come.

At dinner that night Lord Malmesbury had to record that he was 'far from satisfied' with her behaviour as she was 'flippant, rattling' and kept throwing out 'coarse, vulgar hints' about Lady Jersey, who was present. The Prince – with reason now – was disgusted, and this initial feeling of revulsion was later to grow into outright hatred. But there could be no going back on the marriage.

After dinner, he took Malmesbury on one side and asked him why he had given him no warning of what the Princess was like. Malmesbury admitted uncomfortably that the Princess's father *had* told him that the Princess would have to be kept in strict control.

'I see it but too plainly,' said the Prince. 'But why, Harris, did you not tell me so before, or write it to me from Brunswick?'

Malmesbury could only make lame excuses; perhaps the Duke had exaggerated, it had not seemed important at the time, and of course he had been given no latitude to exercise his own judgement. The Prince turned away and left him; there was nothing now to be done.

Malmesbury was certainly very much to blame, but far *far* more to blame was the Queen, who had received a specific warning and did absolutely nothing to save her son from a disastrous marriage.

At the ceremony, Lady Jerningham noted that the Prince of Wales looked 'très morne' and 'twice spoke crossly to his bride'. 'It was expected,' she said, 'that he would have burst into tears.' Their married life was short and ill-tempered, and it was soon so obvious that they were on bad terms that the King wrote to the

Prince to point out that he must not look on his 'disunion' with the Princess as 'merely of a private nature'. His marriage was, inevitably, a 'public act' and he should make every effort possible to keep up appearances and make his home life more respectable. This – naturally – produced little effect on the Prince's behaviour. For the moment, at least, he was less harassed financially, for Parliament, reluctantly and under protest, had increased his income. He had married for money and he had got it, though not so much nor so easily as he had hoped. It was at least something gained from disaster.

All the same, he was far from content with his life. Over and over again, he had begged his father the King to let him have some appointment or office in which he could be useful. Always he had been refused. Once when the King rebuked him for lying in bed so late in the mornings, he had replied with some bitterness, 'I find the day long enough for doing nothing.' When war broke out with France in 1793, he asked at once to be allowed to join the army – to 'addict myself', as he put it, 'to military pursuits'. 'There ought,' he went on—and surely very properly – 'to be some serious object to which my mind should be devoted. . . . To be a cypher in such an hour of glorious exertion would be more than any honourable mind could bear.' The King refused to hear of it. The Prince applied again and again. In 1798 he was still pleading with the King that in this 'serious and aweful crisis' he should be allowed to fight for his country and prove himself 'worthy of the high rank I hold in it by staking my life in its defence'.

In 1803, when war with France broke out again and invasion seemed imminent, he was still begging to be allowed to fight – 'to shed the last drop of my blood in support of your Majesty's person, crown and dignity. For this is not a war for empire, glory or dominion, but for existence.' He could not bear to remain a 'tame, an idle, a lifeless spectator' of the 'mischief' which threatened the country. Once more, he was refused, and he felt himself 'degraded'. In the end, angry, frustrated and perhaps afraid that he might be thought a coward, he took a step which the

King never forgave; he published their correspondence in the *Morning Chronicle*.

He later denied that he had been responsible, but few believed him. 'See what he has done!' said the King. 'He has published my letters.' The King never wrote to him again, and never again did he speak of him but with resentment and disapproval.

IX

Princes of The Blood

George III, true to Hanoverian tradition – a tradition faithfully followed by Queen Victoria in her turn – was consistently hostile to his eldest son. He hated his extravagance, his debts, his frivolity, and the well-advertised dissipation of his life in general. The Prince resented the lack of sympathy he received from his father, extending even to incivility in the small exchanges of social life. He was rude, complained the Prince, when he attended the drawing-rooms, 'speaking to people on each side of me and then missing me, and then, if he does honour me with a word, 'tis either merely " 'tis very hot" or "very cold".'

If it had been only the Prince of Wales who complained of his father, their bad relations could have been put down to temperamental incompatibility or faults of character on the Prince's side; but all his sons complained of the King and his treatment of them is certainly open to criticism. He had been a devoted father when they were young, but his affection for them seemed to evaporate as they grew older. He became brusque and almost cruel, and because he had managed to grow up himself without any exhibitions of wildness, he seemed unable to make allowances for the sort of behaviour natural, or at any rate not uncommon, in high-spirited young men. Also, due to his own Royal Marriages Act, they were placed in exceptionally difficult circumstances so far as their relations with women were concerned. 'Consider what a sad dog a Prince of the blood is,' said Lord Temple, 'who cannot by law *amuse* himself with any woman except a damned German Princess with a nose as long as my arm and as ugly as the devil.

In my opinion a Prince of the blood is the most miserable being in the world.' Lord Melbourne, years later, was equally critical of the Act. It sent the Princes, he said, like 'so many wild beasts into society', making love everywhere they went, and then saying they were so very sorry, but marriage unhappily was out of their power. They had, in fact, been deprived of the right enjoyed by 'all but idiots and lunatics to choose a helpmeet'. Their financial irresponsibility, too, was to some extent the fault of the King, for he gave them unrealistically small allowances when they were young, on which it was probably impossible for them to manage, and at the same time never seems to have seen to it that they were taught to understand the value of money.

Since the King wrote off the Prince of Wales as an incurably debauched character at an early age, it may have been natural to send the next son, Frederick, abroad and so safe from his influence. The experiment, however, seems to have been a resounding failure. He came home with as great an enthusiasm for drink and gambling as his older brother, and was soon involved in a love affair with the Countess of Tyrconnel, whom Mrs Fitzherbert refused to receive on the grounds that she was a 'lady of contaminate character'. Altogether, his reputation was as bad as could be, and Lord Bulkeley dismissed his society as 'mauvais ton'.

Like the Prince of Wales, he was refused all useful occupation except for some nominal military duties, although he would have liked to do more. 'Domestic bliss' seems to have been the King's recipe for boredom and idleness in his sons – he later proposed it, with some lack of realism, to the Prince of Wales when he was pleading to be allowed to join the army – and when Frederick was getting on for thirty, he prevailed on him to marry. Luckier in some ways than his brothers, he knew of a suitable German Princess whom he had actually found attractive. She was Princess Frederica of Prussia, and they were married in 1791. They settled down at Oatlands Park, near Weybridge, and though 'domestic bliss' scarcely describes their relationship, the marriage might

9.   William, Duke of Gloucester, by Wilkie.

10. Frederick, Duke of York, by Wilkie.

be called a modified success. It failed, however, in one of its chief objectives – the provision of a possible heir to the throne.

Frederick was consistently unfaithful to his wife – given the standards of the time and his position in society, it would have been surprising if he had not been – but there was no open quarrel, and, living largely separate lives, they preserved appearances and remained on good terms. She may have been happy enough. She was an eccentric, good-natured woman who seldom went to bed, but spent her nights roaming from room to room while one or other of her ladies read aloud to her. She surrounded herself with a string of dogs, parrots and monkeys – the dogs numbered over forty – but she also became a local Lady Bountiful and was loved by the surrounding villagers.

By 1793, Frederick was once more out of England, for the King, in an access of paternal partiality, had insisted that he should command the British troops in the war with France. He had, after all, spent six years in Hanover learning the arts of war, and now was the time for him to exercise them. Frederick himself was delighted. He had no intention of allowing either his comparative youth or his lack of practical experience to embarrass him in the slightest.

As so often in the history of British arms, the early stages of the war were fought with inadequate forces and a desperate shortage of equipment. Given these handicaps, Frederick did not do badly at first, especially as he suffered the further disadvantage that the Government, angry at his appointment, limited his powers of decision. Of his later failures, too, some at least were the fault of others, though he loyally took the blame. The King was equally loyal to his son, writing him letters of encouragement and telling him to keep up his spirits and remember that adversity is the time to show 'energy of character'.

For a long time the King refused all demands to have him recalled, but this situation of divided responsibility made mistakes very difficult to avoid, and after further reverses, for which Frederick could not be entirely blamed, he was recalled to England at the end of 1794. He was appointed to command again in 1798, but again he presided over a disaster of British arms. His experiences, however, did have one good result.

He had been a brave, if unsuccessful, soldier, and extremely popular with his men; it was a liking which he returned. He had seen for himself how much they had suffered from bad organization and poorly-trained officers and he wanted to make sure that things would be better in future. He founded the Royal Military College at Woolwich for the training of officers, another military college which has since become Sandhurst, and he worked untiringly on measures to provide better care for British troops in the field. The Duke of York, who marched his men 'to the top of the hill' and 'marched them down again' was now transformed into the 'brave old Duke of York'. The memory of his military failures was receding happily into the past and the resounding scandals of the future were yet to come.

It is a curious fact that George III, this supposedly devoted father, seemed always in a hurry to pack his sons out of the country as soon as possible and for as long as possible. William, the third son, had been sent to sea when only thirteen, and it was ten years before he was allowed to settle down in England. Settle down he did, first of all with a girl of the demi-monde called Polly Finch, who left him because she could not endure his reading aloud to her every evening from the 'Lives of the Admirals'. (He always liked to think of himself as a man of the sea and even called his horse 'ships'.) She stood it until halfway through, and then could put up with it no longer.

His next choice was more successful – it was the well-known actress Mrs Jordan, who was said to have a voice 'like honey'. He fell in love with her in 1791, but her feelings for him were rather less impetuous; in fact she made a serious attempt to persuade her current protector to marry her before throwing in her lot with William. When she found he 'shrunk from the test', she decided to choose the protector who 'promised the fairest'; but in practical terms she may have made a mistake. They lived a life of debt, perpetually harassed by lack of money, and she had to keep going out on tour in order to help with the housekeeping.

But they were happy together and lived a cosy domestic life at Bushey until, twenty years and ten children later, William left her in search of an heiress.

He got on better with his father than his elder brothers did, even managing so well, it was said, that George III would actually joke with him about Mrs Jordan; but like his brothers, William resented the perpetual flow of criticism and fault-finding he received from his father. 'My Christmas box and New Year's gift,' he wrote one year, 'will be a family lecture for immorality, vice, dissipation and expense.'

William was an endearing character – bustling, good-natured, and unpretentious. He was often a little foolish and loved to make long, muddled speeches in the House of Lords, startling his hearers with a good word for slavery here, or a stern rebuke for adultery there (characteristically modifying this by a kindly reference to the 'English fair sex' as the 'sources of all endearing comforts in life'). He must have been a difficult man to dislike and Mrs Jordan, even when deserted, never ceased to sing his praises as an 'example for half the husbands and fathers in the world'.

The next son, Edward, took a gloomy view of life from the start. He was born in 1767 when the family was in mourning for the King's favourite brother Edward, Duke of York, and he used to remark in later years that this circumstance was typical of the 'life of gloom and struggle' which awaited him. He always felt hard-done-by, but it is true that, like his brothers, he had a harsh upbringing when once he was past early childhood. At seventeen, he was sent away from England, and it was to prove a very long exile indeed. He went first of all to Hanover to begin his military training, watched over by Baron Wangenheim, an unscrupulous character of fierce disposition who kept for himself the greater part of the allowance of £6,000 a year given him for the Prince's upkeep, and allowed his charge pocket money of only one and a half guineas a week. As Edward said, it was 'open robbery' and no young man of fashion – certainly not a Prince – could have been expected to manage on it.

After five years, he had had enough. He made his escape from the watchful Baron Wangenheim and bolted for England, leaving a mountain of debts behind him. He was affectionately received by his brothers, but not by the King, who refused even to see him, declaring him guilty of 'daring and deliberate disobedience' in having come to England without permission. In the end, after five years of separation, he gave a five-minute interview before packing him off overseas again, this time to Gibraltar.

Here Edward was at least free of Baron Wangenheim and could make arrangements for his domestic comfort. He employed an agent to find him a mistress, and the chosen woman was Mme de St Laurent, the daughter of an engineer of Besançon, who had previously been the mistress of the Marquis of Permangle. Edward was delighted with her – he loved her 'good temper', her 'clever-ness' and above all, her 'pretty face and handsome person'. He had warned her in advance that a 'bed and a few chairs in a cottage' were all that she could expect of life with a simple soldier, but she need not have worried, for this was no way of describing the series of magnificent establishments in which they were to live; all, of course, plunging Edward ever deeper into ruinous debt.

Edward, Duke of Kent, was a man of gentle domestic ways, courteous to women, kind to children; but he was a fiend and a fury whenever his mind was directed to military discipline. The sight of a slovenly soldier drove him wild, and the standards at Gibraltar were notoriously lax. He was soon the terror of the parade ground. Up at five every morning, he inspected, he drilled, he marched his men without respite. And when they failed to come up to his standards – as they were bound to do – he ordered flog-gings of inhuman severity; five hundred lashes, eight hundred lashes. But he was very kind to animals.

When his men were on the brink of revolt, news filtered back to England and he was ordered off to Canada, leaving a crowd of frustrated creditors behind him. He was not to see England for very many years.

In Quebec, he drilled, and inspected, and ordered floggings as vigorously as ever; he had learnt nothing at Gibraltar, except per-haps to order even more atrocious punishments. Driven to desperation, his men laid plans, averted only by luck, to capture and murder him; yet at home with Mme de St Laurent he continued to lead a gentle, civilized life, giving evening entertainments of a sober kind, enlivened only by a little music. He was particularly fond of music and his band of wind instruments accompanied him everywhere.

And still he slid even further into debt; and still he was not happy. 'Why,' he asked, 'should I be left to vegetate in this most dreary and gloomy spot?' Like all his brothers in turn, he longed for England and begged his father to be allowed to return, but quite without avail. In all these years, his father barely troubled to write to him at all. He was given a change of scene by being posted off to the West Indies where he saw action and conducted himself with outstanding bravery; but he was soon back in Canada again, this time in Halifax.

He was as discontented as ever, complaining – and with reason – that it was distinctly hard, after 'thirteen years' absence from home', to be kept in such a 'dreary and distant spot'. The King, it seems, preferred him there rather than at home, so Edward continued with his drilling and his marching. He piled up yet more debts by building a very fanciful establishment indeed, and never ceased complaining about the endless expense of his lost 'outfits'. These 'outfits' were elaborate sets of equipment which, in Edward's case, seemed doomed to come to unfortunate ends – some sold to pay creditors, some captured by the enemy, some lost at sea, and one – a particularly expensive one – sinking beneath the ice of a Canadian lake; and all of them, of course, had to be replaced at ever-increasing expense. They added considerably to Edward's already long list of grievances.

A lucky fall from a horse in 1798, resulting in injuries which his doctor conveniently pronounced only capable of cure by the 'hot pump at Bath', at last gave him an excuse to come back to England; but it was not for very long. Soon he was off to Gibraltar again, this time as governor-general with plenty of scope for his reforming military zeal, for the garrison had once more fallen into bad ways.

'Drunkenness,' said Edward, 'is the bane of the soldier', and he found plenty of it in Gibraltar. He was soon as busy as ever obliging his officers to smell the breath of the non-commissioned officers, and non-commissioned officers to smell the breath of their men before coming on parade. Parades were held early in the morning; the men had to be up at 3.30 in summer and 5.30 in winter, and his officers sometimes even earlier, for they had to visit the barber to make quite sure that every curl was arranged in the precise manner laid down by the Duke. And the punishments were even more fearful than before, one man receiving the maximum penalty of nine hundred and ninety-nine lashes.

He closed fifty of the ninety wineshops on Gibraltar and succeeded in reducing drunkenness to a dramatic extent; he also succeeded, as usual, in bringing his men to the very brink of mutiny and murder. Only a lack of coordination of their planning saved his life. He was recalled to England. And now, at last, he could have stayed there but for the appalling burden of his debts, by this time grown to fantastic proportions. He was forced to consider retrenchment and live what he took to be a life of economy in Brussels – still with his faithful Mme de St Laurent. It was only the necessity of providing an heir to the throne which at last obliged him, after twenty-nine years, to leave her and marry Victoria of Saxe-Coburg, so becoming the father of Queen Victoria.

The King was every bit as anxious to get his fifth son Ernest out of the country as he had been with the others, and he sent him off to the University of Göttingen when he was only fifteen. At nineteen, he was made an officer in the Hanoverian and English armies, and when war broke out he was actively engaged in the fighting. He was outstandingly brave and distinguished himself in battle, but he was twice wounded, and in 1795, when the fighting appeared to have died down, his letters became filled with the familiar pleas to be allowed to come home. He begged the Prince of Wales to do all in his power to help him to persuade his father. 'It will be cruel,' he wrote, 'after such a horrid campaign if the King refuses our coming home.' The King, it seems, was prepared to be cruel, for two months later Ernest was writing again to the Prince to entreat his help. 'I long to return above all,' he said.

One of his wounds had been in his arm, and this was causing him a good deal of pain, but the other wound, which he had received at the battle of Tournai, was more serious. It had damaged his left eye, and from the late summer of 1795 onwards he kept pleading with the King to allow him to return to England for treatment, as he had the 'horrid apprehension of losing it, the greatest of evils'. 'I cannot describe to your Majesty,' he went on, 'how amazingly melancholy and low-spirited this idea makes me.'

Months passed, and the King did not even trouble to reply. Ernest became increasingly anxious. 'I do not know what to do,' he told the Prince of Wales, 'for I cannot sacrifice my eyesight for anything in the world.' The King's silence continued, and in December Ernest was still abroad, still begging to be allowed to return. 'Is it not hard,' he wrote to his brother, 'to have lost the use of an eye in doing my duty and exposing myself for my country, and not to have got as yet an answer from his Majesty, though I have wrote four times?' He had been told that his sight might still be saved if he received the right treatment, and that this could best be obtained in England. 'Now I am determined,' he wrote to the Prince, 'if I do not get an answer from his Majesty, to return without leave, for I will not sacrifice my eye for any whim of others.'

The Prince of Wales, always good-natured where his brothers and sisters were concerned, probably did what he could to help, and at last, in January 1796, Ernest was given permission to come home. The Prince of Wales was genuinely alarmed by his appearance. 'His left eye is shockingly sunk,' he warned the Queen, 'and has an amazing film grown over it.'

It is difficult to find any excuse, or even explanation, of the King's apparent heartlessness towards a son who had fought bravely in battle and whose sight was threatened as a result. Now, apart from the damage to his sight, for which little enough could be done, Ernest was left with a rather ogre-like appearance, which may have had something to do with the ogre-like reputation he was soon to acquire; but not everything. Like Edward, he was never popular with his brothers and sisters and was probably more actively disagreeable. George IV later said of him, 'There never was a father well with his son, or husband with his wife, or lover with his mistress, or a friend with his friend, that he did not try to make mischief between them', and William once remarked rather more pithily, 'Ernest is not a bad fellow, but if anyone has a corn he is sure to tread on it.'

The King, always a hater of innovation, now seemed to have settled into a pattern of behaviour where his sons were concerned. Like his brothers before him, the next son, Augustus, was sent abroad at an early age, for he was only fourteen when he went to the University of Göttingen. Augustus was the delicate member of the family, suffering badly from asthma, and in 1792, when he was nineteen, he was moved to Rome in the hope that the milder climate there would be good for him. It was certainly good for his spirits for it was one of the gayest cities in Europe, and he soon recovered energy enough to fall wildly and recklessly in love.

Lady Augusta Murray, a daughter of Lady Dunmore, was staying at a hotel in Rome when they met. She was considerably older than he was – perhaps by as much as eleven years – but the Prince flung himself at her feet with complete abandon and the most honourable intentions that the Royal Marriages Act would allow him. He wanted to marry her – he was determined to marry her – and he had no qualms about putting his intentions in writing. 'My amiable Goosy', he called her, and declared that his heart beat only for her. He went much further still. 'On my knees before God our Creator,' he wrote, 'I, Augustus Frederick, promise thee, Augusta Murray, and swear upon the Bible, as I hope for salvation in the world to come, that I will take thee, Augusta Murray, for my wife.' Nothing could be more explicit than that, 'And with my handwriting,' he went on, 'do I, Augustus Frederick, this sign, March 21st 1793 at Rome, and put my seal to it and my name.'

Lady Augusta, however, was not entirely satisfied by mere intentions; only a religious service would set her qualms at rest.

It was provided. The Prince managed to find an English clergy-man – the Reverend William Gunn – who was prepared to risk all penalties and marry them. One evening, when Lady Dunmore was out, he and the Prince came to the hotel where Lady Augusta was staying, and the ceremony was performed without witnesses. They were now, as far as they could manage it, man and wife; but not, of course, according to the laws of England.

In the summer of 1793, Lady Dunmore discovered that her daughter was pregnant, rumours of the affair belatedly arrived in England, and in August the Prince was recalled. Shortly after-wards, Lady Dunmore and Lady Augusta followed him and in December another marriage ceremony was performed between a 'Mr Augustus Frederick' and a 'Miss Augusta Murray', this time in the highly respectable precincts of St George's, Hanover Square; but it was still illegal according to the provisions of the Royal Marriages Act.

The King was naturally angry at this reckless behaviour, but he could well have stopped to consider how much he himself was to blame for what had happened. Augustus, still a young boy, had been bitterly lonely and unhappy as he dragged on, year after year, far away from his country and his family, and, like his brothers, always pleading to come home. In one letter to the Prince of Wales, he remarked that he had received a 'few lines' from William which had made him 'very happy' as they were the first he had received in six months from any member of the royal family. On another occasion, he had complained that although he wrote to the King his father once a fortnight, he had heard nothing from him for nearly three years.

In January 1794 a son – Augustus Frederick – was born and two days later the Prince was once more sent out of the country. The King was no doubt anxious to get him away from Lady Augusta, but he may also have been influenced by reports of Augustus's asthma, which was now so severe that he was hardly able to sleep at all. Once he was gone, the King set about having the marriage annulled on the grounds that his consent, necessary to make it legal under the Royal Marriages Act, had never been obtained. The annulment was pronounced that summer and Augustus, exiled in Rome, was frantic. 'My own private peace of mind and honour,' he told the Prince of Wales, 'which are the only two blessings I possess, have been totally ruined. . . . My only desire now is to bury myself in some remote corner of the continent and there to occupy myself about the happiness of her whose misfortunes I am solely the cause of, and the education of my boy. . . . I understand a most arbitrary and unconstitutional promise has been exacted from Lady Augusta never to join me.'

He also worried over her health, but his own was no better for it was 'perishing daily', as he told the Prince of Wales in August 1795, 'and the best part of my life is passing away in a manner as little conciliatory to my honour as to my inclinations'. In the end he was able to circumvent the King's order that his 'wife' should not leave the country and, using a false passport, she joined him in Berlin. Here they lived until 1800 when they returned to England, Augustus still hoping that his father might relent to the extent of giving him a grant and a Dukedom like his brothers. The King, harsh as ever where his sons were concerned, had no intention of doing any such thing, and finally, in 1802, Augustus lost heart and sought an end to his marriage himself, realizing that it would never be recognized.

Adolphus, the youngest surviving son, was unique among the Royal Dukes in living a mild and virtuous life and avoiding all scandal. Although he was said to be the King's favourite son during his boyhood, he was sent out of England at an even earlier age than the others – he was only twelve when he was sent to study at the University of Göttingen in 1786. There he showed himself conscientious in his work and displayed an unusual talent for music.

From Göttingen he went on, when he was sixteen, to join the Hanoverian army and receive his military training. When war broke out with France, he transferred to the English army, saw action, was wounded and taken prisoner, but was rescued. After the usual pleading letters to his father, he was eventually allowed home to recover from his wound.

Here he won golden opinions all round, but he was soon back in Hanover, where he lived for the next eight years as an officer in the Hanoverian army. He rose early, he worked hard, and he practised at his music until he won quite a reputation as an amateur violinist. Here, too, he won all hearts with his delightful manners, entertaining visiting notabilities and becoming an ornament to the social life of the city. Like the happy country which has no history, there is little to say of Adolphus.

There is a lot, however, to speculate upon in the King's treatment of his sons. If it was sensible to remove Frederick from the influence of his older brother, it would seem nothing short of paranoid to feel that all the succeeding brothers as well must be sent away and kept away if they were to avoid contamination. A university education for his sons may well have seemed a good idea to the King, but why always Göttingen? There were universities, after all, in England. And why send them away so young – at fifteen, at fourteen, at twelve? It was perhaps reasonable to feel that they should be given their military training in Hanover, as the training was probably better there than in England, and it was also desirable to forge links with Hanover since it was part of the King's dominions. But why did they have to stay abroad so long? And why did he not write to them, or at least allow them to come home on a visit?

From 1779 to 1785, one after another of his sons was sent away, and kept away, and never seen by choice, for periods ranging from six to seventeen years. To any parent of today it would seem a very great hardship to be so deprived of the company of his children; and it would seem inconceivable to receive letters from a son, such as those the King received from Ernest when he wrote about the danger to his sight, and not even to reply for a considerable time. Ernest commented later, with some bitterness, that it was no use writing to the King for 'the consequence will be his putting my letter into his drawer and no answer will ensue'. All his brothers made similar complaints during the years they spent abroad.

The idyllic picture painted by Mrs Delany of the doting father playing with his young family had changed to something very different. 'Nothing in my eyes is so terrible as a family party,' remarked Ernest, Duke of Cumberland; while on their side, the King and Queen were said to pass 'whole hours together' in tears, worrying over the scandals which beset their children and their generally unsatisfactory behaviour.

Amid these tears and plaints, one wonders whether the King and Queen ever seriously asked themselves if their upbringing of their children might be at least partly to blame. Why did not George III, that ultra-conscientious monarch, sitting up late to write in his own hand his letters of business, take a little more time to keep in touch with his children?

Wellington later made his much-quoted remark that the Royal Dukes were the 'damnedest millstones about the neck of any Government that can be imagined'. By that time, they were. But what had made them like that? There may have been an element of original vice – there was certainly a streak of wildness and eccentricity in the family – but with two such sober and virtuous parents, heredity cannot have been entirely to blame.

George III, in so many ways a kind and good-hearted man, was curiously unfeeling towards his sons. He loved having dear little children to dandle; he was unwilling to undertake the far more difficult task of dealing sympathetically with independent-minded young men. It was much easier to send them away and keep them away.

X

'The Nunnery'

George III may have been cold to his sons but he doted on his daughters. He could hardly bear them out of his sight. Yet the effect this had on their lives was probably more ruinous than anything he ever did to his sons.

He thought them perfection. 'They are all Cordelias,' he exclaimed one day. 'Thank God I have no Regan, no Goneril.' He loved them so dearly that he felt it only natural to want them always with him; from that, of course, it was but a step to deciding that they must not marry. They could not – of course – be allowed to marry commoners, and to marry a foreign Prince would mean that they would have to go and live abroad. It was not to be thought of – it would break his heart. He found no difficulty at all in convincing himself that it would, of course, break their hearts as well.

If this was love, it was as selfish an emotion as could be imagined. One is reminded of the rabbit which eats its young with the kindliest intentions. The strange thing is that although he frustrated their lives and caused them all in turn the most bitter unhappiness, his daughters loved him. They reserved their resentment for their mother who was, after all, merely his accomplice in embittering their lives. 'I never liked her,' said the Princess Royal of her mother. She considered her a 'silly woman', given to 'violence and caprice' in her emotions. 'I was more like a slave than a daughter,' she said in later life. Her sisters all felt much the same about the Queen, and one at least regarded her with outright hatred.

[141]

The Princesses passed lives of almost unimaginable dullness which could only have been made endurable by the prospect of eventual escape. Gradually they came to realize that there was to be no escape for them, and that their lives were to stretch out interminably before them, without change and without hope. The years passed, they grew older, they grew sadder, and still they had to remain at home, still to endure the same dull round, and still, in their forties, to remain under the tutelage of the Queen.

By 1794 the Princess Royal was nearing thirty – a late age for marriage in a Princess – and she was bitterly unhappy. 'She is fallen into a kind of quiet, desperate state without hope,' wrote the politician and poet Sir James Bland Burges, who saw a good deal of the royal family. He thought her 'broken-hearted', and Sir Lucas Pepys even considered her life to be in danger if she were not allowed to marry.

The Princesses were all unusually good-looking girls – Gainsborough, when he saw them, was said to have been driven 'all but raving mad with ecstasy in beholding such a constellation of youthful beauty'. The Princess Royal was perhaps the least good-looking of the sisters, and she took little trouble to make the best of herself. She was clumsy, gauche and painfully shy – particularly when the Queen was present. 'Out of the Queen's presence,' said Mrs Papendiek, 'she was a different being.' Even had she been far less attractive, however, she would not, as the eldest daughter of the King of England, have lacked for suitors. Many offers of marriage were made for her, and a number of them were perfectly eligible; but the suitors were snubbed by the King and their offers of marriage rejected out of hand. It was the kind-hearted Prince of Wales, backed by Lady Harcourt and the Queen's brother, Prince Ernest of Mecklenburg-Strelitz, who came to the aid of the Princess.

Towards the end of 1795, the Prince of Wales was doing his best to persuade Prince Ernest to help him to bring about a match between his sister and Prince Friedrich Ludwig of Oldenburg. 'Ne pouviez-vous pas lui faire sentir que s'il arrivait de demander la Princesse Roiale en mariage, que sa recherche ne serait que bien reçue?' he wrote in enthusiastic, if inelegant, French. He told the Princess of his efforts, and she was delighted – she thought it would be the 'properest situation' for her, and everything seemed to be going well; but in the end, it all came to nothing. Probably the King had seemed upset, and ever since his illness, the slightest sign of agitation on his part was enough to kill off any plan. A relapse was the one thing to be avoided at any cost – this was accepted not only by the Queen but even by the King's ministers in dealing with important affairs of state.

A year later, the Princess's champions were trying again and this time, against all odds, they succeeded. The Princess Royal, in fact, was the only one of the King's six daughters to marry with his consent, and when it came about, she was already thirty years old. The bridegroom was Prince Frederick of Würtemberg, a widower whose wife had been a niece of George III and the daughter of his sister Augusta. The King, as usual, opposed the match and at once pounced upon the fact that Prince Frederick's wife had died – or perhaps even disappeared – in mysterious circumstances. She seems to have been as wayward and indiscreet as her sister Caroline, who was later to be the wife of the Prince of Wales. When she and her husband took up residence in Russia, she proceeded first of all to fall in love with one of the Empress's ex-lovers, and then was tactless enough to give birth to a child long after she had ceased to have sexual relations with her husband. He left Russia, but the Empress would not allow his wife to accompany him, and shut her in a fortress instead. The news eventually reached her family that she had died of a 'putrid fever'. Naturally all sorts of rumours were spread about – that she had been poisoned, that her husband had been implicated in the murder, and even that she had escaped with her lover and was still alive.

'I must decline receiving the gentleman,' was the King's first reaction to this new suitor for his daughter. He then relented to the extent of saying that he might perhaps give his consent if all the rumours were thoroughly cleared up. He probably felt confident that no such thing was possible; but he was wrong. Docu-

[143]

mentary evidence was produced which cleared his proposed son-in-law of having had any part in his wife's death, and the King at last gave his reluctant consent to the match – though causing delays and difficulties to the very end. The Princess Royal was eventually married in March 1797.

Her husband was scarcely a figure of romance. He was distinctly ugly with a large mole on one cheek, and he was so preposterously fat that he was nicknamed the 'Great Bellygerent'. Napoleon later maintained that God had created him to demonstrate the utmost extent to which the human skin could be stretched without bursting. There were slightly discouraging reports about his overbearing temper as well, and other unattractive faults of character. But the Princess was radiant – she had escaped! She was determined to be happy, and it appears that she was. She said so herself, and those who had the opportunity of observing her thought so as well. She even showed her solidarity with her husband by growing very nearly as fat as he was. Her sister Augusta, who saw her in later life, said she would never have known her, she was so 'large and bulky'. 'But what strikes the most,' she went on in a letter to Lady Harcourt, 'is that from not wearing the least bit of corset, her stomach and hips are something quite extraordinary.'

The Princess Royal was the one who got away. The others, for many years to come, remained imprisoned in their spinsterhood and completely in the power of the Queen, who doled them out a little money and controlled them in every detail of their lives as if they had been children. Elizabeth, at the age of twenty-six, once exclaimed happily to Fanny Burney, whose novel *Camilla* had just been published, 'I have got leave! Mama says she will not wait to read it first.'

They had far worse frustrations to endure than having their reading controlled by the prim and censorious Queen. There used to be a comfortable myth of Victorian times that women were untroubled by sexual urges, but the Princesses came of a particularly hot-blooded family. They stayed, perforce, at home, hardly meeting any men apart from their father's equerries, with 'their

11.   Ernest, Duke of Cumberland, by G. Dawe.

12. Edward, Duke of Kent, by W. Beachey.

passions boiling over,' said the diarist Charles Greville, 'and ready to fall into the hands of the first man whom circumstances enabled to get at them.'

Augusta, the second sister, had been rather a tomboy as a child and had enjoyed playing cricket with her brothers. She grew up to be a good-looking and unusually good-hearted, reliable sort of girl, who was glad to help with the education of the younger children. But it was children of her own that she wanted, and most of all, perhaps, a husband.

'I intend for the rest of my life to be very despotic,' she wrote to the Prince of Wales, when she was twenty-five years old, 'till I have a Lord and Master, and then (unless I break the great oaths and promises I shall make when I marry) I shall give myself up to his whims.' She had not yet realized the formidable nature of the obstacles which stood in the way of her realizing the very ordinary ambition of marriage.

Seven years later, in 1799, she fell in love. It was quite hopeless from the start, for the man was a commoner – one of her father's equerries – and the King would never have given his consent to a marriage. It is not *absolutely* certain who the man was, but from various pieces of evidence it seems reasonably clear that he was Major-General Sir Brent Spencer, an exceptionally brave soldier and a good-looking man in a craggy sort of way. Given her state of desperation and her lack of opportunity, she might have chosen far worse.

She was thirty-five when their 'attachment' was 'mutually acknowledged', and she must long ago have given up hope of marrying with the King's approval. She had had a number of suitors, some of them as eligible as could have been hoped. The Prince Royal of Denmark had wanted to marry her, the Prince of Orange had been suggested, and also a cadet of the ducal house of Würtemberg – a young man so charming that nobody could resist him; except, of course, the King, who managed it without the slightest effort, and packed him off home with little ceremony. To another – perfectly suitable – offer of marriage, the King did not even trouble to reply. 'The Princess Augusta,' wrote Sir James

Bland Burges, 'vents her sorrow at her eyes, and cries till she becomes composed and resigned.'

But she was *not* resigned. She chose a man for herself, and may even, with the help of the Prince of Wales, have in the end succeeded in marrying him. Like all the sisters, she adored the Prince – indeed some of her letters to him read more like avowals of passionate love than expressions of sisterly affection. 'Had I time to cover sheets of paper,' she wrote, 'they could never convey how much I love and doat upon you.' And again: 'Toujours présent, toujours cher, that's what you are to your poor Puss. . . . God bless you, ever dearest angel.'

It was to the Prince she turned when at last he was in a position to make it possible for her to marry the man she loved. She had already disclosed to him, some years earlier, the 'secret of my heart', and he had evidently been kind and sympathetic. At that time, however, the King still stood in the way. Now, in March 1812, with the King hopelessly deranged and her brother exercising regal power, she begged him to consider her 'situation'. 'If it is in your power to make us happy, I know you will,' she wrote. She pointed out that hers was 'not a fancy taken up vaguely', but she had known the man for twelve years and they had loved each other for nine. '*Your* sanction is what we aspire to.'

She is evidently afraid of what the Queen will say, for she asks the Prince – should his answer be favourable to her 'Heart's Desire' – to tell the Queen about it himself. 'No consideration in the world,' she writes, 'shall make me take such a step unknown to her. I owe it to her as my Mother.'

Did the Prince Regent give his consent to her marriage? It seems probable, given his unchanging kindness to his sisters and his anxiety to see them married and independent of their mother. There is also one small piece of evidence that he did. A letter of the time, written by the widow of the poet Schiller, who knew some members of the royal family well, states that one of the Princesses had been 'privately married to an Englishman'. Augusta had loved Brent Spencer long and faithfully, and had suffered, as she said, 'martydom from anxiety of mind and deprivation of happiness'. It would be pleasant to believe that she was able to marry him in the end and have at any rate some years of happiness.

Elizabeth, the next sister, is in many ways the most attractive of the Princesses. She had the misfortune to be fat – 'she was born fat,' said Mrs Papendiek, 'and through every illness, of which she had many, she never lost flesh.' It was only partly constitutional, for she seems to have had a remarkable appetite, tucking in to the enormous Georgian meals with hearty enjoyment and sometimes suffering in consequence. On one occasion, she attributed a bout of sickness in the night to a 'remarkable large lobster which I had eat of at supper'. She was nicknamed – not very wittily – 'Fatima'. Fortunately, she did not seem to mind. She was, in any case, a tough-fibred, determined girl who knew what she wanted and was prepared to fight for it. She had a genuine talent for drawing and painting, but she had only one real ambition, and that was marriage; she aspired to be a 'perfect wife'.

There were rumours at the time that she had made a secret marriage in early youth with a 'Mr Ramus', and it is true that there was a family of this name holding various minor appointments at court. It was even rumoured that the frequent 'illnesses' from which she suffered during her twenties were really pregnancies. It is unlikely, however, that these stories of a marriage were true, although she may have had love affairs. She may even have had a child.

The Princess of Wales – not a reliable witness – said that Princess Elizabeth had a child by a 'Mr Carpenter', a son of General Carpenter. According to her, Elizabeth was taken to the house of a midwife for her confinement, but kept herself veiled throughout. When the birth was over, however, she fell asleep and the midwife lifted the veil. At the time, she did not recognize her, but did so later when she saw her at St James's during the birthday celebrations of the King. The Princess of Wales also claimed that her sisters-in-law used to say that as the King had made it impossible for them to marry, they thought themselves entitled to indulge the 'gratifications of matrimony', provided they were discreet. There is another revealing remark attributed to Princess Elizabeth, this time by Lady Sheffield; when they were discussing whether a mutual friend was a virgin or not, Lady Sheffield said 'most certainly' she was, but Princess Elizabeth turned to her sister Sophia and said, 'You know, Sophy, I always say I do not believe there is such a thing as a woman being a virgin, unless she stuff herself with lead.' It has a certain ring of truth, for Elizabeth was inclined to pride herself on her 'Sally Blunt' turn of speech.

But it was marriage she wanted, and she became increasingly unhappy as the years went by and her hopes of escape from the constricted life of the court grew fainter. She tried to be philosophical, 'taking things as they come with patience, tho' sometimes the pill may be bitter to swallow'. In 1808, when she was already thirty-eight years old, she wrote, 'we go on vegetating as we have done for the last twenty years of our lives'.

It was in September of this year that she learnt, through one of her brothers and not from her parents, that an extremely eligible offer of marriage had been made for her. It came from the Duke of Orleans, who later – against expectation – succeeded to the throne of France. She was desperate for the offer to be accepted, but the fact that he was a Roman Catholic added further strength to the automatic resistance of the King and Queen. She herself did not mind in the least. 'On the score of religion, I do not fear it,' she wrote to the Prince of Wales, 'for you know I hate meddling, have no time for gossiping, and being firm to my own faith, I shall not plague them upon theirs.' ('Theirs' meant the Duke.) 'I only entreat of you,' she went on, 'that you will not dash the cup of happiness from my lips.'

She knew that was the last thing she need fear from the Prince, who, as always, was fighting hard on her side. It was no good. The Queen merely said, 'It can never be', and that she wished 'never to hear of it again'. Even so, Elizabeth hoped. The final despair came a week or two later when she made a new discovery. 'I was in such an agony of mind,' she wrote, 'no poor wretch was or has been more miserable than I have. I was all but wild.' She had discovered that 'many many' offers had been made for herself and her sisters in the past which had been refused without their knowing anything about them. 'Therefore we all felt the sun of our days was set.'

Even then, she found the spirit to say she would 'NEVER GIVE IT UP'. And, against all probability, her story has a happy ending. Ten years later, in 1818, when she was nearly forty-eight, even Elizabeth had lost hope. 'All my bright castles in the air are nearly at an end, if not quite so.' Practical and brave as she was, she tried to find consolation in what she had – 'kind and good friends, a great chair, a pinch of snuff, a book, and a good fireside'. With these, she thought, she could 'in the end rest very quietly'.

And then – a most unlikely Prince Charming – the Prince of Hesse-Homburg asked for her hand in marriage. The impression he produced on contemporaries was anything but attractive – 'an uglier hound, with a snout buried in hair, I never saw,' said one. W. H. Fremantle, a Member of Parliament, was even more forthright. 'It is impossible to describe the monster of a man,' he wrote. He was a 'vulgar-looking German corporal whose breath and hide is a compound between tobacco and garlick. What can have induced her nobody can guess.' There was not even money to recommend him, and the Queen was 'outrageous, but obliged to submit'.

She was obliged to submit because although the King was still alive, he no longer ruled; the Prince was by now Prince Regent and, to his sister's delight, he backed the marriage. It turned out as successful as any marriage could be. Behind his unprepossessing appearance, Hesse-Homburg evidently hid a kind heart; and he was, in any case, a *husband* – Princess Elizabeth's 'Heart's Desire'. Tough as always, she did not allow the fact that her mother was dying to delay her marriage, so long desired, and she wasted no time in regretting romance. She easily rose superior to ridicule when her future bridegroom, stooping to pick up the Queen's fan during a ball, 'created a parlous split' in his breeches, and the royal brothers had to make a screen for him while he changed into a spare pair of the Duke of York's. A spirit of unseemly farce pursued them right to the end, for the Prince felt sick in the carriage as they drove off on their honeymoon and he had to get out and sit on the box. But she was married! It was all that mattered. She set off for her new little duchy in June 1818, as happy a bride as could well be imagined.

Four years later, she was able to write, 'I feel so thankful that I am placed where I am. I am so contented with my lot that I can never be too thankful.' And when 'Bluff', as she called her husband, died in 1829, she grieved for him most sincerely. 'No woman was ever more happy than I was for eleven years,' she wrote, 'and they will often be lived over again in the memory of the heart.' And in another letter: 'I can go on hour after hour, thanks to the blessing and pleasure of memory, to look back at the sun beginning to shine upon me, as it did when he arrived, and I am sure it never set afterwards.'

The next Princess, Mary, is the only other daughter of George III known to have married. She was the acknowledged beauty of the family, often described as 'angelic', but she was never really trusted by the others. She was thought to tell tales and pander to their mother. None the less, she was genuinely kind and nursed her younger sister Amelia with outstanding devotion during her last illness.

Like her sisters, she was fretted by the dullness and frustrations of their lives, and resented the minor trials rather more than they did. She particularly hated 'terracing' – that is, parading up and down the terrace at Windsor in the evenings before a crowd of spectators, to the accompaniment of music. It was the custom for a Princess to walk on either side of the King, sometimes for as much as two hours at a stretch, until at last he would touch his hat to the musicians, say, 'Gentlemen, goodnight, I thank you', and retire indoors.

The holidays at Weymouth, she detested equally. 'This place is more dull and stupid than I can find words to express,' she wrote to the Prince of Wales in 1798, 'a perfect *standstill* of everything.' She resented having to get up every morning at five o'clock because that was the hour at which the King chose to rise – a resentment very likely shared by the shopkeepers who also had to get up and open their shops at this unseasonable hour as it was then that they were likely to be 'thronged with all the fashionables at Court'.

Mary was nearly fifty when the question of marriage first arose for her as a serious possibility. The proposed bridegroom was her first cousin Prince William of Gloucester, the son of the King's brother William and Maria Waldegrave. He had shown himself brave in war, but there was little else to say in his favour. He was the original 'Silly Billy' – not William IV to whom the nickname is sometimes attached – and his physical appearance was as unimpressive as his intellectual gifts. He was lanky and shambling, pompous and overbearing, and perhaps as a result of his questionable descent on one side of his family, he put on a tremendous show of royalty. When his shoe came undone at a ball, he made one of his gentlemen, a Major Dawson, kneel down and buckle it for him. Stockmar said he had 'prominent, meaningless eyes', and Charles Greville quoted Dryden's phrase in describing him – 'a lambent dullness plays around his face'.

Yet Mary seemed delighted with the match; in fact, of course, she was delighted with the idea of marriage and independence.

It was not a success, for although William was outwardly pious and full of religious sentiments, he had a streak of cruelty. 'The dear Duchess is not happy,' wrote Creevey, 'and tho' Slice [the Prince] is in politicks a Radical, in domestic life he is a tyrant.' A friend called one day on the Duchess and was surprised to be ushered up several flights of stairs to the very top of the house. The Duchess apologized and said that it was due to the 'cruel manner in which she was treated by the Duke'. He had apparently taken it into his head that the drawing-room suite was not properly cared for, so he had locked up all the rooms on that floor and pocketed the key.

He died in 1834, when Mary was fifty-eight – no great loss to his wife, thought Princess Lieven. 'You will see the Duchess of Gloucester will now get perfectly well,' she wrote in a letter to Lord Grey. 'There is nothing so bad for the health as small daily worries, and nothing so trying as continual ennui.' She was absolutely right.

Mary began to improve in health almost at once and lived for another twenty-three years, dying at the age of eighty-one.

The next Princess, Sophia, was delicate all her life, and is constantly reported as '*very* very ill', or suffering from 'fainting', 'spasms', or 'one of her cramps' – sometimes 'cramps in her stomach', sometimes 'cramp in her head'. Her life was one long tale of illness; at one period, she never left her room for eighteen months. She is, however, the one Princess who is known, almost beyond doubt, to have had a child.

It happened in 1800, and her lover, the father of her child, is generally accepted to have been a General Garth. The unpleasant rumour in circulation at the time, and spread by the Princess of Wales in particular, that the father was her own brother Ernest, Duke of Cumberland, never had much evidence to support it and need not be taken seriously.

At the time, Sophia was twenty-three years old and General Garth was thirty-three years older than she was. He seems to have been an honourable officer, but far from attractive by ordinary standards. He has been variously described as an 'ugly old devil', and 'very plain', and he had, moreover, a disfiguring birthmark spreading from his forehead right over one eye. Princess Mary referred to it once as 'the purple light of love', but it is impossible now to know whether she was merely being facetious or whether she had guessed that her sister was attracted by the General. That might not have been difficult, for Charles Greville had heard that Sophia was so whole-heartedly in love with Garth 'that everybody saw it. She could not contain herself in his presence.'

The affair is said to have begun partly by accident. On one of the occasions when Princess Sophia was unwell, she was moved from the Lower Lodge at Windsor, where the Princesses were living, to the Upper Lodge, so that she could be with her parents. The King and Queen had to go to London one night, and the Princess was left behind. Also left behind was General Garth, one of the King's equerries, who slept in the room directly over Sophia's. Nine months later, a child was born to her at Weymouth.

Somehow – according to Greville – the Princess's condition was kept from the King, who was told that her increasing size was due to dropsy; and he believed it. The problem of course, was to find some explanation for her sudden return to her normal figure when the child was born. Eventually the King was told that she had recovered from her dropsy by means of the 'roast beef cure'. 'This he swallowed,' maintained Greville, 'and used to tell it to people all of whom knew the truth, as a "very extraordinary thing".' Extraordinary indeed.

It was all but swallowed by Sophia herself, if Caroline, Princess of Wales, is to be believed, for she told Lord Glenbervie that Princess Sophia was 'so ignorant and innocent as really not to know till the last moment that she was with child'. Glenbervie wondered whether she could really not have been aware that 'something particular' had passed between herself and General Garth. As he remarked reasonably enough, it was not a matter 'as indifferent and as unlikely to have consequences as blowing her nose'. The Princess of Wales also told Glenbervie that the 'foundling' was left at the 'Taylors' house in Weymouth—this probably referred to Sir Herbert Taylor, who was later Private Secretary to the King. General Garth acknowledged the boy, and – perhaps the one happy feature of this rather sad little story – came to love him dearly. In fact, he doted on him to excess. Sophia seems to have visited the boy from time to time, but in the end he turned out badly, and even attempted to blackmail the royal family.

It was the one major event, the one act of rebellion, in Sophia's long life of invalidism. There were rumours that she may have gone through some ceremony of marriage with General Garth, but if so, it made little difference, for she never lived with him openly and he remained a bachelor.

Amelia, the youngest Princess, was, like Sophia, an invalid from an early age, but, unlike Sohpia, she died young. And she, too, had her sad little romance with a perfectly respectable, perfectly eligible man from the point of view of his personal qualities, but a man whom – as she very well knew – the King would never permit her to marry.

At fifteen she developed a tubercular infection in her knee, and from that time onwards she was never really strong, although her letters show her to have been a lively and spirited girl. She loved the Prince of Wales, called him Eau de Miel, and wrote to him in terms of great affection, as all the sisters did. 'Why did you leave this place so soon?' she wrote from Weymouth in 1797. 'Oh! fie! You don't know how sorry I was when you went; indeed I was.' But there was an odd little postscript. 'I wish the wind would go down; it hurts the drumsticks of my ears.' She suffered always from nervous tension and a tendency to melancholy in addition to all her physical ills.

The following year, the Prince was writing about her to the Queen in some anxiety. 'Her appetite is shocking, and if she goes to force it at all, her stomach throws up in a very short time afterwards what she has swallowed. . . . She likewise has a most dreadful cough which, whether nervous or not, still is very unpleasant.' It was a cough that was to persist.

For the time being, however, she improved a little and was able to lead an almost normal life at Weymouth, even bathing in the sea. Here, in 1801, her family left her when they went back to London, so that she might have the benefit of the bathing and the bracing air a little longer. She was now nearly eighteen. Among those who remained behind with her was her father's aide-de-camp, Colonel the Honourable Sir Charles FitzRoy. In some ways, he had more to recommend him than General Garth – he was younger, for one thing, though still twenty-two years older than she was, and he was generally admitted to be good-looking in a rather wooden sort of way. He had neither dash nor charm, however, and seems to have been on the frigid side into the bargain. It was the lively, passionate Princess who made all the running.

She loved him to madness. His letters have been lost, but hers remain – adoring, anxious, spiked with fear that perhaps she has annoyed him in some way, or even – dreadful thought – that he does not truly love her. He seems to have allowed himself to be wooed. 'Do sit in Chapel where I can see you,' she begs. 'Do have your dear hair cut and keep it for me.' He is her 'own dear angel'. Her doting glances began to be noticed, as was the way she would drop behind when out riding so that she could talk to him.

The affair persisted, passionately pursued by the Princess, sedately accepted by the Colonel. In 1803 Miss Gomm, who had helped Miss Goldsworthy to look after the Princesses when they were children, began to be worried and warned the Queen of what was going on. But the Queen preferred to be ignorant, so long as unpleasantness could be avoided. She referred to what Amelia regarded as the great love of her life as 'this unpleasant business' and merely asked her to promise never to mention it 'directly or indirectly' to her brothers. Above all, she must say nothing to the King as it would 'make him unhappy, and make our home very unhappy'. There is an implied threat that she might unbalance the King's mind.

The association went on as though nothing had happened. 'I glory in our attachment,' wrote Amelia. And on another occasion, 'Oh God, how I love you! I have loved you from the first I sought you, and blessed be God – I gained you!'

As the years passed she became increasingly dissatisfied with the state of affairs between them. It is not quite certain whether they became lovers or not, but even if they did, Amelia was not satisfied; it was marriage she wanted. 'Marry you, my own dear Angel, I really must and will. . . . Oh good God why not be together? I pine after my dear Charles more and more every instant.' At times she found it difficult not to become depressed – particularly in 1804 when the King was once more seriously ill. 'God knows I am more wretched than I can express, and I see no end to it,' she told the Prince of Wales. 'Could an Extinguisher fall upon the whole family I think, as things are, it would be a mercy.'

Yet she had now begun to cherish a gleam of hope for the future. She had obtained possession of a copy of the Royal Marriages Act and had studied it carefully, and she now realized that when she was twenty-five – that is to say, in 1808 – she would be able to marry FitzRoy legally, *if* she could obtain the consent of the Privy Council, and Parliament made no objection. From 1804 onwards, she took to signing her letters 'A.F.R.' (for Amelia FitzRoy) and had this monogram engraved on her silver. It is possible that she may have gone through some sort of ceremony with FitzRoy in anticipation of the formal union which she now saw as a practical possibility – in fact, a near certainty whenever the King should die. She was confident that the Prince of Wales would never stand in the way of her happiness.

In 1807, Miss Goldsworthy and Miss Gomm once more warned the Queen. They were worried in case they should be blamed for what was going on and had been alarmed to receive an anonymous letter accusing them of conniving at Amelia's love affair. A 'sad row' ensued; but still the Queen was chiefly concerned with keeping up appearances rather than with her daughter's unhappy situation. She wrote to Amelia – who had, after all, loved FitzRoy unswervingly for at least seven years – exhorting her, somewhat unrealistically, to 'subdue at once every passion in the beginning', and not to be 'a disgrace to yourself and a misery to all who love you'.

Was the Queen among those who loved her? It may be doubted. Two years later, when Amelia was once more seriously ill and was being nursed by Princess Mary in Weymouth, she had become convinced that the Queen was her enemy and did not wish her to recover. 'I don't expect much feeling or pity in that quarter,' she wrote. And after her return to Windsor, she complained of the Queen's cruelty; 'but now I can't stand it,' she added. It may have been to some extent a fancy bred of her illness, for she was now very ill indeed. Even sleep brought her no relief, and after a 'good night', she would complain that she had dreamt, as usual, that she was in pain.

She grew rapidly worse, and although she herself sometimes hoped that she might live, it was plain that she was dying; but her dislike and distrust of the Queen never relaxed and she wanted her to be kept out of her room as far as possible. Princess Mary even felt it necessary to write to the King: 'Any harshness in a sharp *word* goes very deep with her, and if she is so situated as to be liable to have those coming in and out she cannot with any propriety refuse to see, I cannot answer for the consequences.' Apparently the Queen had been complaining that Amelia was selfish in monopolizing Mary's time and attention. 'If that is ever said to Amelia,' wrote Mary, 'you must perfectly understand it will *half kill her.*'

It is significant that the King made no attempt to question Princess Mary's opinion, but made arrangements for Amelia to be moved to Augusta Lodge, Windsor, a house which Dr Heberden, one of the King's physicians, had formerly occupied. Amelia's illness dragged on through the summer of 1810, but in October, the King – who was ill himself by this time – was still managing to hope; or at least trying to convince himself that she would not die. 'You are not uneasy, I am sure, about Amelia,' he said abruptly one day to Miss Cornelia Knight, a lady of the Court. 'You are not to be deceived, but you know that she is in no danger.'

Hardly more than a week later, Amelia was dead. She was only twenty-seven years old.

And so the youngest of the Princesses died, full of bitterness, full of hatred against her mother and maintaining to the end that 'anxiety and ill-usage' were largely responsible for all she had suffered.

The unhappiness of these six princesses, lasting over so many years, is almost unbearable to contemplate. George III is, of course, chiefly responsible, but his faults were more human and understandable than those of the Queen. He genuinely loved the Princesses, even though in a limited and self-indulgent way, and it was beyond his scope to make the imaginative effort required to realize that their feelings and wishes might be very different from his own. Every time the question of marriage for one or other of them was raised, he became intensely distressed and never failed to find some good reason, satisfying to himself if nobody else, why the marriage was undesirable. He had also the excuse of his own serious illness of 1788. As one instinctively protects an injured limb, he may, almost unconsciously, have tried to shield himself from emotional stress. He always blamed his various breakdowns in health on some worry or strain to which he had been subjected.

It is much more difficult to understand the Queen's indifference to all that her daughters were suffering; and worse than indifference. She actively intervened to prevent them from marrying. At first she had the excuse that she must safeguard the King's mental equilibrium, and that that was paramount. If she *had* to choose between the welfare of her husband and that of her daughters, there is at least a case for saying that she was entitled to put her husband first. Unfortunately, it seems likely that it was her own peace of mind with which she was chiefly concerned. She had been badly frightened by the King during his illness of 1788, she had detested the publicity and all the squabbles about the Regency, and she was determined that nothing of the sort should happen again if she could possibly prevent it.

Yet it cannot have been pleasant to live surrounded by these resentful, angry and increasingly desperate daughters. They had all told her at one time or another how much they wished to 'settle', and unless she was completely heartless, she must have felt some compassion for all that they were going through. On the other hand, her son Edward, Duke of Kent, said that she had a 'natural want of warmth', and a friend of Princess Amelia, who had plenty of opportunity of observing the Queen at close quarters, felt sure that she 'never had one grain' of 'parental affection' in her composition. It is perhaps significant that when she wrote to Amelia about her affair with FitzRoy, she warned her against making 'our home very unhappy', but she says nothing of Amelia's unhappiness.

Even in 1818, when the King's health could no longer be her excuse, she still fought as hard as she could to prevent Princess Elizabeth's marriage. She wept, she blustered, she would have none of it, and she was actively rude to her daughter's suitor. 'My mother is a spoilt child,' said Elizabeth. In the end it was only through the persuasions of the one child she undoubtedly did love – the Prince of Wales – that she was brought round to a grudging consent.

It was convenient to her, of course, to have her daughters always on hand to bear her company and do small errands for her; or perhaps she was unconsciously revenging herself on them for the frustrations of her own life. It cannot have been an altogether happy life – married at seventeen to an immature young man, forced to live a lonely, dull existence among foreigners and to bear fifteen children in quick succession. She may have felt she was doing her daughters a favour in protecting them from a similar fate, and she may well have developed an antipathy to sex and its consequences. In later life, she certainly showed herself determined to avoid sexual relations with the King.

She gave no sign of wishing to be on intimate terms with her daughters, and she may not have cared that none of them really liked her, none of them trusted her, and that one of them died, hating her to the last. She was an enigmatic woman, she betrayed nothing; 'that little dear word silence' was still her 'constant companion', and she seemed to withdraw ever further into herself.

XI

Disorder and Disarray

The first ten years of the nineteenth century brought George III much trouble and anxiety both in his public and his private life. He went through an acute emotional crisis in 1801 as a result of the Government's proposal to make some reduction in the disabilities from which Roman Catholics still suffered; they were not, for instance, able to vote, or to sit in Parliament, or to hold public office of any kind. Pitt, in particular, felt it to be very important that at least *something* should be done for them – especially in view of the current troubles in Ireland – but the King had convinced himself that any change whatsoever would involve the violation of his coronation oath.

So strongly did he feel about it that he gathered his family about him at Windsor and read the coronation oath aloud to them. 'Will you,' it ran, 'to the utmost of your power maintain the laws of God, the true profession of the Gospel, and the Protestant reformed religion established by law?' He then asked them if they had understood what he had read. They assured him they had. 'If I violate this oath,' he told them, 'I am no longer sovereign of this country but it falls to the house of Savoy.'

Pitt, on his side, held to his views every bit as strongly as the King and declared that his government had no alternative but to resign if they were prevented from introducing reforms which they considered vitally necessary. The King was distressed but unmoved.

'Where is the power on earth,' he asked, 'to absolve me from the due observance of every sentence of that oath, particularly the one requiring me to maintain the Protestant reformed religion? Shall I be the first to suffer it to be undermined, perhaps over-turned? No, I had rather beg my bread from door to door through-out Europe than consent to any such measure.' The Lord Chan-cellor, Lord Eldon, attempted to reason with him, and argued that the King could not be held to be breaking his oath if the measure were duly approved by Parliament. The King would have none of it.

'I can give up my crown and retire from power,' he said. 'I can quit my palace and live in a cottage. I can lay my head on a block and lose my life, but I cannot break my coronation oath.'

Some of this extremism and passion may perhaps be interpreted as the first symptoms of oncoming illness, but it was none the less true that the King had always felt very strongly about his duty to maintain the constitution. Lord North once said of him that he 'would live on bread and water to maintain the constitution of this country', and it is at least possible that the extreme anxiety he felt about the Roman Catholic question may have sparked off, rather than been a symptom of, a new breakdown in health.

By February 1801, the King was definitely unwell, with much the same physical and mental symptoms as in his illness of 1788. He had cramps, constipation, colic, muscular pains and racing pulse. He had begun to talk too much and was so low-spirited that he was liable to burst into tears. And once again he had begun to speak of Lady Pembroke – by now elderly as well as formidably virtuous – in terms of passionate physical love. He was determined, he said, to go to her. Once again the Prince of Wales behaved with a curious lack of heart for one so capable of affection, and at a concert given by Lady Hamilton he even remarked casually to the French diplomat M. Calonne, 'Savez-vous que mon père est aussi fou que jamais?'

The King had some awareness of his own state and of its dangers. 'I have prayed to God all night,' he said, 'that I might die or that He would spare my reason.' His prayer was not answered, and by the end of the month Dr Willis was once more on the scene. This time, however, it was not the father, who was by now eighty-three years old, who was in charge, but his two sons. 'Must I put on the waistcoat?' asked the King philosophically, but he was assured that he need not.

At the beginning of March, there seemed to be some sort of crisis, and according to Lord Malmesbury, the King's 'life was despaired of'. However, he fell into a sleep from which he woke seemingly normal, and from then on, he continued to improve. By 7 March, he was able to say to the Duke of York, 'I really feel quite well, and I *know full well* how ill I have been.'

The King now instructed Dr Willis to go to Pitt and tell him that he was now 'quite well, QUITE recovered' from his illness. 'But what,' he went on, 'has *he* not to answer for who is the cause of my having been ill at all?' Poor Pitt was so upset by this message that he at once wrote to the King to say that he would no longer insist on pressing for a change in the law regarding Catholics. 'Now my mind will be at ease,' said the King. However unintentionally, his illness had turned out to be a neat piece of blackmail. It effectively prevented his government for the next ten years from bringing in a reform which they not only thought advisable, but urgently necessary.

The King's illness had been a trying time for his family and at the drawing-room of 26 March it was remarked that the Queen looked pale and the Princesses 'as if they had been weeping'. The Prince of Wales was observed to behave 'very rudely' to the Queen, and the troubles of the family were increased by the slowness of the King's progress towards complete normality. Dr Willis was still in attendance in May, and he reported to the Lord Chancellor that although the King would often claim to have had a 'most charming night', the Queen told a very different story. On 25 May, for instance, he had spent the night, so the Queen told Dr Willis, in 'restlessness, in getting out of bed, opening the shutters, in praying at times violently. . . . He frequently called out, "I am now perfectly well, and my Queen, my Queen has saved me".'

If it was an anxious time for the King's family, his ministers also had their worries, for how was public business to be carried out if the King was unable to sign papers? This presented no problem at all to Dr Willis, who helpfully said that he would obtain the royal signature to any amount of papers. The ministers, however, were far from reassured, for relying on Dr Willis was tantamount, so they thought, to putting 'executive government in the hands of that gentleman'.

The King, more worried than any of them at the continued surveillance of Dr Willis, at last broke out into downright re-bellion. He had been living at Kew, separated from his family, in the company of Dr Willis and his brother the clergyman, but he now told Lord Eldon that he had made a 'solemn determination' that unless he were allowed to go and visit the Queen that very day, 'no earthly consideration should induce him to sign his name to any paper, or do any one act of Government whatever'. Lord Eldon agreed that it was certainly right for him to visit the Queen, and from that time the King rejoined his family. By June 1801, he was even well enough to go for a holiday at his favour-ite Weymouth, in spite of unenthusiastic reports from Dr Willis.

Lord Malmesbury saw the King in October, and thought him 'rather more of an old man' than he had been, but he was rational enough. He talked of the peace with France, which he called an 'experimental peace', and of which he did not approve. When Lord Malmesbury tried to turn the conversation to more neutral subjects, the King interrupted him.

'Lord Malmesbury,' he said, 'you and I have lived on the active theatre of this world these thirty years; if we are not become wise enough to consider every event which happens quietly, and with acquiescence, we must have lived very negligently.'

War with France broke out again two years later, and the King, brave as ever, said he would like to 'fight Bony single-handed'. 'I should give him a good thrashing, I'm sure I should – I'm sure of it,' he declared. He made arrangements for the Queen and his daughters to go to a place of safety, as the French were preparing to invade, but he declared his own readiness – at sixty-five years of age – to lead his troops in battle. 'If the French should effect a landing,' he said, 'I shall certainly put myself at the head of my troops.'

Active service in defence of his country was a privilege he was still denying the Prince of Wales in spite of all his pleadings, and it was in 1803, either from anger at his father's obstinacy or in order to vindicate his own courage, that the Prince had allowed the letters which had passed between them to be published in the Press. Soon afterwards the King is said to have asked Compton, one of his pages, whether he had any children.

'Yes,' replied Compton.

'Sons or daughters?'

'Only daughters.'

'Never have any sons,' said the King. 'If you have, there must be an eldest, and he will publish your letters.'

The King's health was once more breaking down, and this time the strain seemed to be more than his family could endure. They were frightened of him and his strange, wild behaviour, which made him so utterly unlike himself. He began to use indecent expressions, even before the Princesses, and once, while on board his yacht at Weymouth, he addressed a lady of the party with the words, 'Dear, lovely Mrs Drax, what a pretty ass you have got! Bring it here. How I should like to pat such a pretty ass!' The King said this in a loud voice which 'reached every part of the ship', and it amused the sailors so much that they 'tumbled over one another into the hatchways, unable to retain their fits of laughter'. It was all very unlike the usual behaviour of the normally strait-laced King.

He once again reverted to his old passion for Lady Pembroke, and the Princess of Wales began to spread mischievous stories about him. She told Lady Glenbervie that he had taken 'freedoms' of the 'grossest nature' when he had visited her, and on one occasion he had made such a 'sudden and violent attempt on her person that it was with the greatest difficulty she escaped being ravished by him'. None of this may have been true, but there was no disguising the fact that the King's mental balance was seriously upset.

In June 1804, Pitt wrote to the King begging him to put himself under medical care, but the King had taken an even stronger dislike than ever to doctors since his experiences of 1801. He may have had reason, for he once confided to Lord Eldon that one of the men employed by the physicians to look after him had knocked him down. 'When I got up again,' added the King, 'I said my foot had slipped and ascribed my fall to that; it would not do for me to admit that the King had been knocked down by anyone.'

During his illness of 1804, the King seemed able to talk to his Ministers in a reasonably collected manner, and to control his eccentricities in public life, although Lord Glenbervie does record the rather charming story that the King, on his way to open Parliament, told his companions that he meant to surprise the two Houses at the beginning of his address. 'I mean to say, "My Lords and Peacocks",' he declared.

'Surely your Majesty would not use that expression!' exclaimed one of his attendants.

'Yes, I shall,' said the King. 'I shall certainly say "My Lords and Peacocks".'

Glenbervie himself thought the story untrue, but it gained so much currency that people would often say, 'I am going to see what the Peacocks are doing', when they were on their way to Parliament.

The King was at his worst in private life and he took to dismissing his servants quite capriciously, even including his favourite page, Braun. He also removed the Queen's coachman and — what was 'more serious because more notorious' – he dismissed Lords of the Bedchamber 'without a shadow of reason'.

His family were bitterly unhappy, and the Queen, in particular, turned against him. She refused to see him except in the company of one of the Princesses, and she locked her bedroom door against him. The Cabinet begged her to allow the King to share her room, but she would not hear of it. She had had enough, she would make no new efforts. 'It is a melancholy circumstance,' said Lord

Hobart, 'to see a family that has lived so well together for such a number of years, completely broken up.'

George III once again recovered his mental balance, but the years ahead were to be full of anxiety for him. A cataract formed over one eye, and the sight of the other was threatened. As usual, he was brave. He told Mrs Harcourt that there had been a time when he used to say that if he ever lost his sight he would wish to die, but he now realized how wicked that was. He was trying hard to reconcile himself to the idea of blindness and to 'think of resources when the misfortune happened'.

In 1806, there was unpleasant publicity to be faced when the Prince of Wales, hoping for a divorce, asked the King to allow an investigation to be made into the alleged adultery of his wife with Rear-Admiral Sir Sidney Smith. She had given plenty of cause for scandal, often getting up in the middle of a dinner party and disappearing for hours on end with one of her male guests, and some of her remarks were extraordinarily indiscreet. 'I have a bedfellow whenever I like,' she said on one occasion. 'Nothing is more wholesome.'

The Commission which carried out the 'Delicate Investigation', as it was called, came to the conclusion that adultery had not been proved, but that the Princess's conduct had lent itself to 'very unfavourable interpretations'. The King, who had given her some support until now, wrote and told her of his 'concern' and 'disapprobation', and forbade the Queen and his daughters to have anything more to do with her; but this, of course, was not much help to the Prince.

Within three years, the Duke of York was in trouble. He had always remained on good terms with his wife, the eccentric Princess Frederica, but naturally he had had mistresses, and by 1803, in the steady manner characteristic of the Hanoverians, he had settled down in a domestic kind of way with a Mrs Clarke. She was a woman of low birth and little education, but quick-witted, intelligent and amusing. She was also very good-looking. The Duke was entranced by her and wrote her impassioned letters whenever they were apart – letters that were later to achieve an embarrassing publicity. Unfortunately, Mrs Clarke was extravagant as well as charming, and soon the Duke began to be worried by the size of her debts. He at last realized that if he continued to live with her, he might be involved in a major scandal, and even jeopardize his position as commander-in-chief of the army. So – with great reluctance – he told her she must go. This was in 1806. He promised to pay her an annuity of £400 a year, but unfortunately – more unfortunately for him than for her as it turned out – he neglected to do so.

She became very angry at this treatment, and threatened to publish his letters, but he ignored her threats and nothing more happened until she met Colonel Wardle, the Member of Parliament for Okehampton. They saw quite a lot of each other and he encouraged her to boast about the influence she had, so she said, exercised over the Duke of York in the appointments he had made in the army. Wardle had a personal interest in all she had to tell him, as events proved.

On 27 January 1809 Colonel Wardle rose in the House of Commons and moved that a committee should be appointed to investigate the conduct of the Duke of York, in particular with regard to 'appointments, promotions, exchanges, the raising of new levies and the general state of the Army'. There had been corruption, he affirmed, and he was determined to expose it.

It was bound to be a popular cry, and the government overreacted. Instead of appointing a committee, which was all they had been asked to do, they declared that the matter should be investigated in the most open way possible, and should therefore be brought before the bar of the House. In other words, every squalid detail of the Duke's relations with Mrs Clarke, as well as any embroideries she might care to invent, were to be discussed in circumstances of the utmost publicity.

The proceedings lasted for seven weeks and Mrs Clarke had the time of her life. 'The woman is very clever,' said Lord Temple. She was caught out in lie after lie, but was so witty in her repartee that everybody was entranced with her and her sayings were quoted all over London. So were the Duke's love letters. 'How can I sufficiently express to my Sweetheart, my darling love, the delight which her dear, pretty little letter gave me,' he wrote in one of them, 'Millions of thanks for it, my Angel.' People no longer called 'Heads or Tails' when tossing a coin, but 'Duke or Darling'.

Mrs Clarke made it clear that she had taken money over and over again in exchange for promises to influence the Duke in making promotions in the army, but the question which remained unanswered was whether she did in fact influence him; and – more important still – did he know that she was taking money? There was no real proof that he did and Lord Eldon, the Lord Chancellor, assured the King that the evidence before the House 'did not establish any charge of corruption'.

The Duke now sent a letter to the Speaker of the House formally declaring 'in the most solemn manner on my honour as a Prince' that he was innocent. A vote was taken in Parliament and by a majority of 278 to 196 the Duke was found not guilty of corruption. In spite of this, however, he took the view that since such a large number of the members of the house had apparently believed he had 'connived at the sale of promotions' in the army, he must resign as commander-in-chief. He now behaved very well. Without fuss, and without complaint, he went away to live quietly with his wife at Oatlands.

The King had been greatly upset by the scandal and all the unseemly revelations, but he was to have no period of respite, for within a year there was a new scandal, this time involving another son, Ernest, Duke of Cumberland. Cumberland had a sinister reputation, partly caused – and most unfairly – by the evil appearance which had resulted from the wound to his eye; 'our little bit of glory', as Princess Augusta had called it at the time. He was a distinctly disagreeable character, however, always stirring up trouble, and the general public had had no difficulty in believing him – again unfairly – to be the father of his sister Sophia's child.

On 30 May 1810, the Duke, who was living in St James's Palace, went to a concert. His valet, Sellis, helped him to dress and was then sent away for the night. After the Duke had gone out, the housemaid removed the cushions from the Duke's bed, as usual, and put them away in a closet in another room. She laid the bell-pull over the end of the bed and closed all the shutters in the state apartments which adjoined the Duke's bedroom. The Duke's sabre, which had recently been repaired and sharpened at Sellis's suggestion, was lying on the sofa in the bedroom. Later, this maid was to say that she thought she had heard someone creeping through the state apartments while she had been making ready the bed.

The Duke returned from his concert at about half past twelve, and was in bed and asleep by one o'clock. Suddenly, he received two violent blows on the head. He put out his hand for the bell-rope, failed to find it, and received two more blows as he was trying to get up. The room was dimly lit by a lamp which had been left burning, but the Duke was unable to see anybody, and he staggered towards the door leading to the room where his page, Neale, was sleeping. He shouted, 'Neale! Neale! I am murdered,' and the page, still half asleep, came running into the room barefoot. He trod on the sabre which was later found lying on the floor of the ante-room between his own room and the Duke's.

Neale supported the Duke to a chair, the sentries and the sergeant on guard were called in, and they began a search. The Duke kept asking for Sellis, and a servant was sent across the court to the apartments where he normally slept with his family. He was not there. One of his children said that he was sleeping in the Duke's apartments that night, so the steward went to the door of the room which Sellis sometimes occupied. It was locked, but a gurgling noise could be heard coming from inside.

The Duke still kept asking for Sellis, and the page – Neale – remembering that there was another door into Sellis's room, set off to see if he could open it. As he passed through the state apartments, he noticed that the upper shutters of the windows were now open.

This second door into Sellis's room was found to be unlocked, and Neale went inside accompanied by the porter. Sellis was lying back on his bed, 'his hands on each side of him, and his face composed'. He was dead. 'Good God!' cried the porter, 'Mr Sellis has cut his throat.'

There was a blood-stained razor lying near his hand, and a basin containing water reddened by blood was on a table near-by. His coat – heavily stained with blood – was hanging on a chair at the other end of the room. Since it was clearly impossible that Sellis could have hung it there *after* cutting his throat, it was obvious that it must have been stained with blood before he took it off.

The sequence of events seemed clear. Sellis had attacked the Duke, and had escaped through the state apartments. (A smear of blood on the frame of the door leading into them exactly corres-ponded with blood on the sleeve of Sellis's coat.) He had then begun to undress – one of his 'half-gaiters' was off, when he was found, and the other unbuttoned – but he had been disturbed by the knocking at his door. Realizing that his crime was bound to be discovered, he lost his nerve and cut his throat.

Further proof of his guilt later came to light. He had told the housemaid the evening before that he was sleeping in the Duke's apartments because the Duke was leaving for Windsor next day and he had to be on hand to attend him. He had told his wife the same story. It was not true – the Duke had had no intention of going to Windsor and no other servant had heard of it. In addition, one of Sellis's slippers was found in the closet where the cushions from the Duke's bed had been placed, together with a bottle of water. Neither had been there when the maid had put the cushions inside. Sellis had evidently made his way through the State apartments while the Duke was out, and had stayed hidden in the closet until he judged the Duke must be asleep.

At the inquest, a verdict of suicide was brought against Sellis, and it was agreed that there could be no doubt that he had attacked the Duke. The motive was more obscure. It came out later that Sellis would often abuse the royal family, and was par-ticularly bitter against the Duke of Cumberland because of the heavy-handed jokes he made about Sellis's religion. (Sellis was a Catholic.) He also resented the fact that he was, apparently, the Duke's favourite servant and was always called to attend him in preference to anybody else.

The Duke's injuries were serious, for the blows on his head had exposed the brain, and his right thumb was almost severed; but they won him little sympathy from the general public, who, in spite of the evidence, now believed him a murderer as well as the father of his sister's child.

For the King, there was worse to follow, for it was about this time that it became clear that Amelia, for so long gravely ill, was dying. 'She is absolutely going out like a candle,' said the Princess Augusta. During these last months of her life, the physicians would report to the King every morning at seven o'clock, and at frequent intervals during the day, and he would sometimes keep them for over an hour, examining them minutely about every detail of her condition. He went to see her every day as well, but these visits were strictly controlled and were never allowed to exceed five minutes. His sight was by now so bad that he could scarcely see her, and he would bend down over her and peer into her face, searching pathetically for some signs of returning health. There were none. By October, Amelia had given up all pretence of hoping that she might one day get well, and she gave the King a ring which she had had specially made for him. It contained a lock of her hair enclosed under a crystal tablet and set round with 'a few sparks of diamonds'. She placed it on his finger, saying, 'Take this to remember me.' It was too much for the King. He hurried from the room, 'overpowered with grief', and never entered it again. A few days later Amelia was dead.

The King had once written to his friend Bishop Hurd of Worcester, 'I place my confidence that the Almighty will never fill my cup of sorrow fuller than I can bear'; this last grief he could not bear. His reason had been precariously balanced for some time, and now he lost his last frail hold on reality. For a few days, he could still collect himself, and he was even able to make the arrangements for Amelia's funeral, choosing the anthems himself; but even so, he would still assure people about the court that he knew very well that Amelia could be 'brought to life again'.

This delusion settled on his mind, and soon he was convinced that Amelia was alive and living in Hanover where 'she would never grow older and always be well'. He even attempted to console one of his physicians, whose wife had recently died, by assuring him that she, too, was in Hanover; soon he had the long-dead Prince Octavius there as well. Hanover, in fact, seemed to have become a synonym in his mind for heaven.

The darkness was thickening and soon he was to lose all touch with the world, and with reality.

XII

'An Uncommon Degree of Benevolence'

Early in 1811 it became obvious that the King could no longer transact public business and the Prince of Wales must be appointed Regent. The appointment was to be for a year only and the same limitations on his powers were to be imposed as had been agreed in 1789, but this time the Prince accepted them philosophically. The King, too, was resigned to the situation, and when the Bill was brought to him, he gave his assent, merely remarking that it was no more agreeable to him to be turned out of office than it was to any other man.

During the year, the King's state of mind fluctuated, and for a time the physicians were optimistic about his eventual recovery. In the summer, he even had a brief period of near-normality when he was able to walk on the terrace at Windsor just as of old; but it did not last, and he was soon drifting away on a tide of all his old fantasies, including even his ancient passion for Lady Pembroke, now in her seventies. At times he thought he was having a love affair with her, at others he believed she was his wife.

'Is it not a strange thing,' he said to his son Adolphus one day, 'that they still refuse to let me go to Lady Pembroke although everyone knows I am married to her; but what is worse, that infamous scoundrel Halford [one of the royal physicians] was at the marriage and has now the effrontery to deny it to my face.'

By February 1812, it had become clear that there was to be no recovery for the King this time. His son, William, had been to see

[173]

him a little before this, and had reported that although he ate 'with appetite roast mutton, took his broth with turnips and bread and cheese with pleasure', he was far from normal mentally. There was, said William, an 'absolute vacuum of mind'. The Prince Regent assumed full powers in February 1812 and among his very first acts was the promotion of a Bill aimed at securing some measure of independence for his sisters.

An annuity of £30,000 had been secured to the Princesses in 1802, but they were only to receive it in the event of the King's death. The Regent now desired that some money should be made over to them immediately, and that the House of Commons should 'enable his Royal Highness to make such provision for their Royal Highnesses the Princesses as . . . may be thought suitable to the actual situation of the Princesses'. After some discussion, it was agreed that the four unmarried Princesses should receive pensions of £7,912 1s. 9d. each, which were to be paid to them direct and not through their mother. They were no longer to be dependent on the Queen.

They were ecstatic; she was not. She was, in fact, beside herself with anger. Independence for her daughters was the very last thing she wanted and she fought it to the end. She had done nothing to help them during their long years of repression, and it seemed that she had no intention of letting them go now, even though she could no longer make the King's state of mind her excuse.

The Princesses had suffered severely during these last years. The Queen had spared them nothing. They had been obliged to act as unwilling buffers between the King and their mother so that she could carry out her resolve never to be left alone with him, never to sleep with him again. Night after night, they had been obliged to stay at her side, in the unsympathetic role of gooseberry, until at last the King went off angrily to bed and they were released. And since the King's mind had become permanently unbalanced, they had had to live in the gloomy atmosphere of Windsor, hearing his 'unpleasant laughing' ring through the house, visiting him, and sometimes witnessing his uncontrolled behaviour, his occasional violence. They were scarcely allowed to escape even for a day, even for an evening, from the oppression and gloom. The Queen had pronounced that 'under the present melancholy situation of your father, the going to public amusements . . . would be the *highest mark of indecency possible*'. Even visits to their brothers were frowned on as liable to lay them open to scandal.

She could not endure that they were now to be free to regulate their own lives, and she was not in the least mollified when they wrote her a joint letter promising that she should never be left alone and that they would show her every mark of duty and affection. She sent them a furious reply ending with the statement that she did not wish to see any of them that day 'for I do not think I ever felt as shattered in my life as I did by reading your letter'. She never seems to have considered for one moment that the oldest of the Princesses was now nearly forty-four and the youngest in her thirties.

The Queen had fought the Prince's plan from the moment she heard of it, even 'storming down to Oatlands', where the Prince was staying at the time, and 'tormenting' him, although he was seriously ill, in an effort to prevent his giving the Princesses an independent establishment. The Princesses, however, showed themselves as determined as she was, and somehow managed to put up with all the rows, and the scenes, and the endless reproaches.

'We have neither health nor spirits,' they wrote in a joint letter to their brother, 'to support for any length of time the life which we have led for the last two years, more especially the treatment which we have experienced whenever any proposal has been made for our absenting ourselves for a few days from the Queen's roof, either with a view to that relaxation which it is natural and we trust not unreasonable at our ages we should occasionally seek, or in compliance with the expression of your pleasure repeatedly conveyed to us.'

A particularly 'dreadfull scene' followed an act of defiance on the part of two of the Princesses in accepting an invitation from the Prince of Wales to visit the House of Lords in spite of the Queen's opposition. The Prince, trying to soothe his mother, wrote to say he had been most 'deeply afflicted' to hear of the angry scene. 'I do implore you, my dearest Mother,' he went on, 'for your own happiness, for that of my sisters, and for the peace of the whole family, not to suffer the repetition of scenes so distressing.'

The Queen wrote an unyielding reply saying that she felt it 'more decent' that the Princesses, in 'their situation, as personal witnesses of the distressing situation of their father', should 'decline appearing in public'; besides she objected to being left 'almost all alone', as she seemed to think she would be if ever two of the Princesses went on a brief visit to London.

She then gave the Prince her own version of the scene with her daughters.

'I will not deny,' she wrote, 'that the answer I received from Mary when I found fault with her . . . provoked me to the quick, for she assured me she could no longer lead the life she had led, and that Sir H. Halford was of the same opinion, and when Elizabeth, by defending her own conduct, struck upon a book, saying she had done all in her power to please, it provoked me.' She particularly resented the 'telling me that living with me in my distress is disagreeable'. She would never forgive them, she said.

In spite of these painful scenes, the Princesses remained deeply grateful to their brother for coming to their rescue, and Sophia, who had always been delicate and had now sunk into semi-invalidism, even roused herself to write him a letter, to which she gave the bitter heading 'From the Nunnery'.

'As I know how difficult it is for you, my ever dearest brother, to read my scrawls,' she wrote, 'I am determined to send you a few lines in a legible hand, trusting to your kindness to forgive my troubling you at this busy time, but my heart overflows with gratitude for all your noble and generous intentions towards us which, should you succeed or not, our *gratitude must be the same*. The only thing that frets and worries me is the idea that your kindness to *four old cats* may cause you any désagrémens with the Ministers. I could forfeit everything sooner than that we should be the cause of this. How good you are to us, which, however imperfectly expressed, I feel most deeply. *Poor old wretches* that we are, a *dead weight* upon you, *old lumber* to the *country*, like *old clothes*, I wonder you do not vote for putting us in a *sack* and *drowning us* in the Thames. *Two* of us would be fine food for the fishes, and as to Miny [Mary] and *me*, we will take our chance together. . . .'

'How good' he was to them indeed, and they loved him for it. 'Neither my pen nor my words can ever tell you half how I love you,' wrote Princess Elizabeth. And at last the storms died down, and the Princesses were able to enjoy their limited freedom.

The Queen remained bitter and morose, with 'cross words' and 'sour looks'. The lively girl, playing the harpsichord to her seasick companions, had become unrecognizable in this harsh and ageing Queen. She had had much to endure – she still had – and it was bound to affect her character. But she had her virtues – she gave very generously indeed to charity, and her gifts had the extra merit of being secret. Yet she did not have a generous spirit – she was, in fact, rather mean. On one occasion, during a visit to Weymouth, she bought up in advance the entire stock of goods which were to be offered at sale prices by a local draper. The housewives of Weymouth were furious, and the shopkeeper hardly less so, for it had been a strictly cash offer and the Queen delayed paying for some considerable time. She dearly loved a bargain. She often used to send a servant to buy books cheap from the market stalls, saying, 'I have a servant very clever; oh, it is amazing what good books there are on stalls!' It was a trait not very sympathetic in a Queen.

She was a strictly 'virtuous' woman, in the narrow sexual sense, but in judging others, her standards were uneven. It seemed to be largely a question of being found out; a divorced woman would be treated as unfit to associate with, while Lady Jersey, notoriously the Prince's mistress, was received in a friendly way at court.

Perhaps her worst fault was that she lacked 'natural warmth',

M

as one of her sons said of her, and almost the only person, apart from the Prince of Wales, to whom she ever showed real affection was the King, and that was during the early days of their marriage. Some of her letters to him have a certain charm and spontaneity. 'I cannot refuse myself,' she writes, 'the agreeable occupation of beginning to scribble by way of conversing with him who takes up the greatest part of my thoughts.' And again: 'A thousand thanks unto you for your kind affectionate letter which arrived last night by a quarter past ten after my commerce party was broken up. It hath served me as supper and is to keep me company at breakfast.' But she deserted him in the end, and after 1804 they lived largely separate lives, preserving only the façade of unity.

In those early days, she was also capable of showing a dry sense of humour, as when she said to one of her ladies, 'The English people did not like me much because I was not pretty. But the King was fond of driving a phaeton in those days and once he overturned me in a turnip field, and the fall broke my nose. I think I was not quite so ugly after that.'

But peevishness and dissatisfaction had settled on her as the years passed and her 'bad temper' seems to have been accepted as a family problem. 'It was the object of the dear King's life,' wrote Princess Mary, 'to keep from the world *all* he *suffered* and *went through* with *her temper*.' And Prince William once remarked that his father had 'married a disagreeable woman', but had not 'behaved ill to her'.

The King was, indeed, extremely loyal to the Queen and never spoke against her, but it may be that marriage to this plain, narrowly virtuous, cold-natured woman added one more strain to those he already had to endure and may have contributed to his breakdowns in health. The historian A. D. Greenwood said of Queen Charlotte that she will be remembered as an example of the harm which may be done by a good woman.

From 1810 onwards, the Queen did her duty as she saw it, regularly visiting her husband in his suite of rooms on the ground floor at Windsor, but always accompanied by the physicians and one or other of her daughters. She did her duty, but not, apparently, with grace; according to Princess Mary, 'her unfortunate manner makes things so much worse', largely, she thought, because of the Queen's lack of 'warmth, tenderness and affection'. After 1812, she seems to have left the duty of visiting the King largely to her daughters.

The King drifted further and further away from the real world, and as he did so, his physical health improved. He ate with a good appetite, chiefly his favourite roast mutton and cherry tart, but his mind was clouded. There were moments, however, when he seemed to realize his situation. 'I must have a new suit of clothes,' he said one day, 'and I will have them black in memory of George III, for he was a good man.'

At last darkness and silence overwhelmed the King. He was completely blind, and at the end, almost completely deaf, yet music was still, in some sense, a consolation to him. Sometimes he would feel his way to the harpsichord placed ready for him in every room and stop to play a favourite passage from one of Handel's oratorios, remarking that he had been 'very fond of it when he was in the world'. But for the most part, wearing a dressing-gown of blue velvet, with the star of the Order of the Garter pinned to it, he would pass his days wandering restlessly from room to room, pausing to address dead friends of long ago, or haranguing statesmen in their graves these many years. Occasionally the old hurry and press of speech would come upon him, and then he would push his handkerchief into his mouth until it was bitten through.

He had one interval of complete lucidity in the summer of 1814. The Queen entered his apartment and found him singing a hymn and accompanying himself on the harpsichord. Suddenly he knelt down and prayed that it might please God to take his 'heavy calamity' from him; or, if not, to give him the resignation to bear it. Then he burst into tears.

'The gleam of reason fled', and the world receded. In November 1818, Queen Charlotte died, and he knew nothing of it; the storms of battle and war and crisis raged outside, but he was untroubled. It seemed that he might live for ever. And then – almost abruptly – he relinquished his hold on life. He began to refuse his food – it was as though, in some deep recess of his being, he had decided that he had had enough. He grew quickly weaker and he died – at the end quite peacefully – on 29 January 1820.

'The decease of a good old King . . . will leave a deep impression of sorrow,' wrote Lady Sarah Lennox, whom he had loved long ago. 'I cannot help thinking of the poor King today.' Dull, limited, selfish and obstinate, utterly infuriating as he must often have been, he was still – over-ridingly – a good-hearted man.

'He always had more than a common degree of benevolence,' wrote Mrs Harcourt, 'and a love of contributing to the happiness of those around him.' It makes a kindly epitaph.

Select Bibliography
Index

Select Bibliography

ACKNOWLEDGEMENTS

I have been most grateful for the invaluable collection of royal
letters made by A. Aspinall: *The Later Correspondence of George
III* (5 volumes) and *The Correspondence of George, Prince of Wales*
(8 volumes); also *Letters from George III to Lord Bute* edited by
Romney Sedgwick. *The Letters, Diaries and Journals* of Horace
Walpole and the *Diary and Letters* of Mme d'Arblay (Fanny Burney)
are, of course, of first-class importance for the period in general,
and the privately printed *Harcourt Papers* for the private life of
George III and his family. Robert Greville's *Diaries*, covering the
period 1788–9, give much the best non-medical description of the
King's illness, and Mrs Papendiek's reminiscences provide a vivid
impression of life at court from a close, but rather different, point
of view.

Roger Fulford's charming book *Royal Dukes* is most valuable
and illuminating; also *The Daughters of George III* by D. M.
Stuart and *The Romance of Princess Amelia* by W. S. Childe-
Pemberton, which contains a number of family papers published
for the first time. *The Hanoverian Queens of England* by A. D.
Greenwood is still irreplaceable, and among modern biographies
I have particularly enjoyed *George the Third* by Stanley Ayling.

Allen, W. Gore, *King William IV* (1960)
Aspinall, A. (editor), *Later Correspondence of George III*, 5 vols
——, *Correspondence of George, Prince of Wales*, 8 vols
Ayling, Stanley, *George the Third* (1972)

Berry, Paul, *By Royal Appointment* (1970)

Brooke, John, *King George III* (1972)

Buckingham and Chandos, Duke of, *Memoirs of the Courts and Cabinets of George III*, 4 vols (1853–55)

Burges, Sir James Bland, *Selections from the Letters and Correspondence*, ed. J. Hutton (1885)

Burney, Fanny (Mme d'Arblay), *Diary and Letters*, 6 vols, ed. C. F. Barrett (1904–5)

Chandos, J., *Criminal Conversation* (radio script)

Chapman, Hester, *Caroline Matilda* (1971)

Childe-Pemberton, W. S., *The Romance of Princess Amelia* (1910)

Creevey, T., *Papers*, ed. Sir H. Maxwell (1903)

Croker, J. W., *Correspondence and Diaries*, ed. L. J. Jennings (1885)

Delany, Mrs, *Autobiography and Correspondence*, 3 vols, ed. Lady Hanover (1862)

Derry, J. W., *The Regency Crisis and the Whigs* (1963)

Dobree, Bonamy, *Letters of King George III* (1935)

Dodington, G. Bubb, *Diary* (1785)

Duff, David, *Edward of Kent* (1938)

Fitzgerald, Percy, *Dukes and Princesses of the Family of George III* (1884)

——, *Life and Times of William IV*

Fulford, Roger, *Royal Dukes* (1933)

——, *George IV* (1935)

Glenbervie, Sylvester Douglas, Lord, *Diaries*, 2 vols, ed. Francis Bickley (1928)

Gillen, Mollie, *The Prince and His Lady* (1970)

Green, J. R., *History of the English People* (1898)

Greenwood, A. D., *Hanoverian Queens of England* (1911)

Greville, Charles, *Memoirs*, 4 vols, ed. Henry Reeve (1888)

Greville, R. F., *Diaries*, ed. F. McK. Bladon (1930)

The Harcourt Papers (privately printed)

Hervey, J., Lord, *Some Materials for the Memoirs of the Reign of George II*, 3 vols (1931)

Hibbert, Christopher, *George IV. Prince of Wales* (1972)

Huish, R., *Public and Private Life of George III* (1821)

Iremonger, Lucille, *Love and the Princesses* (1958)

Jerningham Letters, 2 vols, ed. E. Castle (1896)

Jesse, J. H., *George the Third*, 3 vols (1867)

Keith, R. M., *Memoirs and Correspondence* (1849)

Knight, Cornelia, *Autobiography* (1861)

Lennox, Lady Sarah, *Life and Letters*, 2 vols, ed. Countess of Ilchester and Lord Stavordale (1901)

Leslie, S., *George IV* (1926)

Long, J. C., *George III* (1960)

Macalpine, I., and Hunter, R., *George III and the Mad Business* (1969)

Malmesbury, J. Harris, Earl of, *Diaries and Correspondence*, 4 vols (1844)

Marples, Morris, *Poor Fred* (1970)

Martin, Sir T. Byam, *Journals and Letters*, ed. R. V. Hamilton (1903)

Melville, Lewis, *Farmer George*, 2 vols (1907)

Molloy, J. Fitzgerald, *Court Life Below Stairs* (1882)

Murray, Hon. Amelia, *Recollections* (1868)

Namier, Sir L., *Personalities and Powers* (1955)

Neale, Erskine, *Life of Edward Duke of Kent* (1850)

Nicolson, Harold, *The Age of Reason* (1960)

Papendiek, Mrs C., *Court and Private Life of the Time of Queen Charlotte*, ed. Mrs Vernon Delves Broughton (1887)

Parreaux, A., *Daily Life in England in the Reign of George III* (1969)

'Pindar, Peter', Poems, various. End of eighteenth and early nineteenth century (various dates)

Plumb, J. H., *The First Four Georges* (1956)

Postgate, R., *That Devil Wilkes* (1956)

Quennell, P., *Samuel Johnson* (1972)

Robertson, C. G., *England Under the Hanoverians* (1911)

Rose, G., *Diaries and Correspondence*, 2 vols, ed. L. V. Harcourt (1860)

Sedgwick, R., *Letters from George III to Lord Bute* (1939)

Sheridan, Betsy, *Journal*, ed. William le Fanu (1960)

Stockmar, Baron, *Memoirs* (1872)

Stuart, D. M., *The Daughters of George III* (1939)

Taylor, Sir H., *The Taylor Papers*, arranged by Ernest Taylor (1913)

Taylor, Joseph, *Relics of Royalty* (1820)

Thackeray, W. M., *The Four Georges* (1872)

Thraliana (The Diary of Mrs Thrale), ed. K. C. Balderston (1942)

Trench, C. V., *The Royal Malady* (1964)

——, *George II* (1973)

Turner, E. S., *The Court of St James's* (1959)

Twiss, H., *The Public and Private Life of Lord Eldon*, 3 vols (1844)

Vulliamy, C. E., *Aspasia* (1935)

——, *Royal George* (1937)

Waldegrave, Earl, *Memoirs* (1821)

Walpole, Horace, *Memoirs of the Reign of George III* (1845)

——, *Journal of the Reign of George III* (1859)

——, *Letters*, ed. P. Toynbee (1918–25)

Wardroper, J., *Kings, Lords and Wicked Libellers* (1973)

Watkins, J., *Memoirs of Charlotte, Queen of England* (1819)

White, T. H., *The Scandal-mongers* (1952)

Wilkins, W. H., *Queen of Tears* (1904)

Wilson, Sir Robert, *Life*, 2 vols, ed. H. Randolph (1862)

Withers, P., *History of the Royal Malady* (1789)

Wraxall, Sir N. W., *Historical and Posthumous Memoirs*, ed. H. B. Wheatley (1884)

Yorke, P., *Correspondence of Princess Elizabeth* (1898)

Ziegler, P., *King William IV* (1971)

Index

Index

Index

Index